UNION SQUARE

A Novel

Adrian Koesters

Apprentice
House Press
Loyola University Maryland

First Edition

Printed in the United States of America

Hardcover ISBN: 978-1-62720-192-6
Paperback ISBN: 978-1-62720-193-3
E-book ISBN: 978-1-62720-194-0

Design & Development by Rachel Kingsley
Marketing by Alessia Hughes
Author Photo by Eugene Selk

Cover photo used with permission from *The Baltimore Sun,* made possible by the generous support of Trif and Stacey Alatzas.

Published by Apprentice House

Apprentice House
Loyola University Maryland
4501 N. Charles Street
Baltimore, MD 21210
410.617.5265 • 410.617.2198 (fax)
www.apprenticehouse.com
info@apprenticehouse.com

Advanced Reviews

"In her debut novel *Union Square*, author Adrian Koesters brings to life the hardscrabble residents of a once grand neighborhood. Its denizens take us with them Rashomon-style through a single weekend, Thursday through Palm Sunday. Their often violent lives intersect in richly mysterious ways: a would-be Irish prizefighter ruins his prospects in exchange for the satisfaction of beating up a neighborhood rival. A recluse who can barely get out the door of his house finds himself hopping trains to help rescue the beaten boy. A girl on the cusp of adolescence falls in and out of love hourly, her physical and emotional turmoil carrying her into real danger. The place, the people, and the moods of an era are vividly evoked by Koesters' gifts for visceral detail, dark humor, and the most forgiving sort of empathy. Scenes from this deeply evocative novel will stay with you like strange and unforgettable images from your dreams."

— Mary Helen Stefaniak, author of *The Cailiffs of Baghdad, Georgia*

"*Union Square* is about neighbors and neighborhoods, about the play of light and shadow, about spiritual connections made and lost. Honest, haunting, refreshingly idiosyncratic. I was captivated by the novel's balance of nostalgia and gritty realism, and fascinated by the lives of these characters navigating prejudice and fear."

— Timothy Schaffert, author of *The Swan Gondola*

"It is rare to find a debut novel written in such beautiful, lush prose and yet packing such a powerful punch that you feel as if the world has been knocked off its axis. Adrian Koesters shines as a brave new fiction talent in *Union Square*, a story that reverberates with rawness and truth-telling as a family confronts the darkness of its own secrets against the backdrop of the corruptions in their community. Koesters' breathtaking lyricism shines on every page, lifting the characters and the reader beyond the darkness of their story toward the redemptive hope of connection."

— Jonis Agee author of *The Bones of Paradise*

"I loved this book. It is flat-out the best thing I've read in several years, and that includes a number of award-winning novels. I hardly know how to describe the experience of reading it. Koesters reminds me of Virginia Woolf in her atmospheric power and ability to convey interiority, of Hemingway in her clarity and punch, and, once-in-a-lovely-while, of Cormac McCarthy in her syntactic drive and her swooping dives into metaphysical brooding. She gets everybody, from cocky-but-yearning teenage boys to psychically shattered, violent young men to snarky, guilty old pedophiles to heartbreakingly innocent young girls torn between desire and God. Really—if you have another novel you've started, put it aside and read this one. The other one will wait. This one will pin you to the wall."

— Kent Meyers, author of *Twisted Tree*

UNION SQUARE

A Novel

for Jay Bates
and
Boyd W. Benson

"Baltimore was as far a place as you could go with those you loved, and it was where they left you."
– Eudora Welty, *The Optimist's Daughter*

"I said, 'Hey, Carmen, come on, let's go downtown.'
"She said, 'I got to go, but my friend can stick around.'"
–"The Weight"

Contents

Union Square, Baltimore, Thursday, April 3rd
to Sunday, April 6, 1952

Part One: Carmen.

Thursday Morning: Good-bye, House of Good Shepherd

Carmen Stunchen was not in bed. As she leaned into the glass of the front window, peering out from the third floor over to Union Square, she was thinking of Mr. H. L. Mencken, on his Hollins side of the park, who had sometime opined that, "Conscience is the inner voice that warns us somebody may be looking," and she was trying to see over to his house. It pleased her that he lived there. All she knew about him was that he was famous, she didn't know why or what for. Really, she thought that it was a shame he was so old and, what they said, so ill. She wanted to believe he looked down into the square at night, and she wanted to know that when she was there, he was looking at her when she strolled, or sat, or much later at night when no lights were on and no police patrolled. She would agree with this observation Mencken made, misunderstanding him or perhaps not altogether.

Otherwise she wasn't noting much else in particular. She was beat. She could hear her seven-year-old daughter, Lucille, crying in the next room. She supposed Mr. Morris had hit her or something. He had slept, but he woke, and when he woke after staying the night always wanted to get down to things, but Carmen was not interested in his foolishness first thing in the morning, definitely not on her living room couch. She had sent him off to the bathroom to make himself a little more respectable, if possible.

The sun peels over the row houses on the right-hand side of the park, she thinks, and watches the slowness of its light begin to fill up Union Square. Through the day, the clean, weak sunlight will pass over the tarred lengths of the roofs, slide over the straight moldings, and a block away stagger downhill. The sun will light up the House of Good Shepherd on the west and the brick fronts of Hollins and Lombard Streets on the north and south. Over the day it will heat up the square, seduce flower bulbs, slide down the buildings, cross the street, and by evening once more make what length it can up the fronts of the eastern houses before releasing doorways and steps and sidewalks to darkness, disappearing for good finally into the west.

A cupola shades the drinking fountain. She can't see the flowers that emerged yesterday afternoon, but they have already had it. She can't see the few dozen cigarette butts and the square bottle thrown into one of the hedges, but she sees them in her mind. A gentleman composed mostly of grey shoves his way in the semi-dark across the diagonal of the square block of park, and Carmen thinks from the shape of him that she knows him, or that she'd like to know him.

H. L. Mencken is in fact in his house, ending his life on one side of the park, but he doesn't come into this story. Here afternoons littered with white children running to and from schools, here alleys and back streets with Negroes invisible to the whites, but not to her. She doesn't care about any of that, though—she wouldn't use the word *shit*, but it was just that to her, boring, stupid, she wouldn't pay it any mind. She had given herself that luxury a long time ago.

This light that travels the row houses from east to west on Union Square, even into the small windows of its basements, *This*, she thinks, *this is perfect*.

She's hungry. She tries to peer again through the trees in Union Square over to Hollins where Menkle or whatever his name was, but it's too far to get a good look. Aside from being old and sick, he was rich, that she knew. He'd lived there forever. She needed some money, and she wished she could go over and ask him for some, but she was going to have to go to her mother's for it instead, and who knew if she'd even give it to her. Well, she'd cross that bridge when she came to it.

She lifted her shoulders in a luxurious gesture. Her house had been broken up into apartments and the streets around the square were starting to show signs of age, but for her they could never be less than distinguished, these brick fronts and marble steps that had all been rich at one time, better than anything you could find anywhere, she bet.

She had been frightened of the place when she was younger, frightened of the sisters who went in and out of the House of Good Shepherd, the home for wayward girls, a place her mother threatened her with but where she had never had to go because she had married Mr. Morris, Donna and Lucille's father. He lied and said she was sixteen instead of fifteen, and this Menkle, he had lived on the opposite corner to the Sisters the whole time, his whole life just about, and now she lived here, too, and the Sisters couldn't get her now no matter what she did. The year it was, even, had a lovely ring to it. Nineteen-fifty-two. The war and all, it was over. Things were going to get better and better.

But she was broke.

She heard Lucille crying again and called out, "Be quiet in there!" Mr. Morris laughed through the wall and said something, but she couldn't make it out. She heard Mr. Morris in the bathroom after that, moving around. She walked through, saw Lucille in bed with her face turned to the wall. "Oh, good," she thought, "she'll get some sleep." Donna, the elder girl, was on the trundle next to Lucille's bed, her eyes wide open, staring at the ceiling.

"Good morning, Glory," Carmen said with a little laugh, "you're sure up early."

She reached for the pack of cigarettes that was on the top of the dresser. Donna transferred her gaze from the ceiling to her mother but didn't speak.

Mr. Morris came out of the bathroom at a trot, stopped when he saw Carmen, smiled broadly and swatted her on the fanny, said, "I'm starving—let's go out and get something."

"Sure, handsome," Carmen said, "but let me get myself put together once, would you, for a change?" She said this with a laugh, and then, as though there were only the two of them in the room, began a slow strip-tease of the already brief garments she had on. Donna closed her eyes but didn't move. Mr. Morris howled and clapped and slapped his knees as if Carmen had been up on stage down on the Block. Someone from the house next door banged on the wall.

Thursday Noon: You Wouldn't Give Your Two Cents Worth

Carmen twisted the gold-plated rhinestone ring on her engagement ring finger, waiting for Miss Maurice to come back into the kitchen. There was a pitcher of home-made wine on the table. Miss Maurice made the wine up in the bathtub and put it into glass bottles and stored them down in the cellar, but she always had a pitcher of it sitting on the kitchen table, and when Carmen had been a little girl and had stayed there very often, she'd run by, take a dipper of wine and drink it, and then run out again to play. Later she would say that she didn't remember a time when she hadn't been at least slightly tipsy, but at the moment she was not in the mood to drink anybody's homemade wine. She wanted a stiff shot, but she wouldn't find that here. She twisted at the ring again and then knew it might come down to the wine in a minute after all.

She was in one of the most broke periods she could remember for a good while. She easily found jobs and as easily lost them: she'd work for six weeks or three months, and then she'd get caught with someone's hand up her skirt, or hers in the cash box, and that would be that. She'd moved the girls umpteen times since they were babies and after Mr. Morris had left them mostly permanently, until her mother had had enough of it, the moving in and out and the squabbling and the babies crying, and told her that she'd pay the rent on an apartment, and by luck she'd found the one on Union Square, where she was, damn it all to hell, going to stay until they put her in the cold ground. The landlady and the neighbors didn't know she was part this and part that, and she wasn't going to tell them. But those girls were driving her crazy, she was out of work again, and she needed something besides homemade wine and polite white boys.

Miss Maurice wasn't Carmen's relative, though her nephews, nieces, and godchildren littered the length of Lemmon Street. Miss Maurice's parents had named her what they had thought was one of the prettiest names they had ever heard, and it wasn't until she was well into her teens that someone mentioned they thought it might be a man's name. She'd had trouble collecting insurance benefits from her husband, a Mr. Buddy Jackson, whom no one, including Carmen's grandmother whose best friend she was, had ever met, and who had been almost all white and had worked as a porter on the B & O his entire life. After he died, the company was shocked to meet this nearly coal-black woman claiming to be his wife, and wouldn't give out benefits without proof that her name was indeed Maurice. But she had a birth certificate and a baptismal certificate, and she took the monsignor from St. Peter Claver with her to halt any other funny business they might think up. He witnessed her signature, and she and Carmen's grand-mother lived on the money in high style. Carmen was glad to get back to her house on Lemmon Street, plain but lavish in feeling, quiet and dark, small and real, the house where she had stayed off and on all through her childhood and into her teen years.

When Carmen was a little girl her mother would drop her off for the day and Miss Maurice came to the door without any-body having to knock on it. From her face anybody could have told you she had spent her life not giving a damn what anybody thought about anything, what Carmen loved about her. Skinny, her sparse hair oiled back and pinned in a tiny bun at the back of her head, she wore out-sized costume earrings of rhinestones set in a gaudy circular pattern, and there was always a pair of read-ing glasses hanging from a chain on her large chest. Her nose was small, as if someone had smashed it into her face above lips that when she was thinking pursed into a duckbill shape Carmen walked around imitating. Miss Maurice continually worked her tongue over her large, bow-shaped mouth, and it was this per-fect mouth that made you wonder just how old she really was. Carmen knew she was well into her seventies, maybe older.

Carmen's grandmother, Carmella Stuncheon, who had been as black as Miss Maurice was herself, had lived with Miss Maurice after Mr. Jackson died, and had died herself some years previously. Carmen's mother had been the one to hold the threat of incarceration at the House of Good Shepherd for what had seemed like an infinity of years, and it would be her mother, white as a sheet, who was now in the living room playing cards with Miss Maurice and the other ladies at the canasta game. But it would be Miss Maurice who would come back out to the kitchen and give Carmen a little something to tide her over.

"Why, hello, child!" she'd cried down to her from the front door as she had done since Carmen was little. Carmen had to step down a stair when she opened the door. "Oh, my goodness, look at you, you're froze to death. Get on in here and get yourself warmed up in the kitchen. We're playing cards."

Preamble was unknown to Miss Maurice, as was conjecture about past and future. In this, she and Carmen were strangers to the other.

Miss Maurice and Carmella, for whom Carmen had been named, had had in their years together a peculiar way of keeping the Sabbath holy, and that was to go to the earliest Mass at St. Peter Claver and then to spend the rest of the day cooking, eating, playing cards, and drinking fruit wine and beer. They kept a poker game going from about noon until everyone left sometime between eight and ten at night, and then played canasta together with a dummy hand until midnight promptly. They shut the cards down, checked all the stoves in the kitchen and the locks on the front and back doors, and went to bed, most often separately but sometimes together, "Just for a little cuddle," Miss Maurice would put it, raising her eyebrows at Carmella.

"Just a little one," she'd say back and wink, "right after I soak my dentures."

Since Carmella's death, Sundays had remained poker day, but a canasta game now seemed to go on perpetually every other day of the week. "Hey, Olivia, look what I got," Miss Maurice had said to Carmen's mother, shoving Carmen like a little girl into the door of the parlor where six ladies were hunched over the card table or leaning back in their chairs. "She looks like she's about to expire from chill. I'm going to set her in the kitchen and get her some tea and something to eat."

"Don't give her no money," Olivia said, not looking up from her hand.

"Lord, that woman is hard," Miss Maurice muttered, pulling Carmen by the elbow. "There's days I miss your grandmother so much I could spit."

Carmen didn't touch the plate of cookies Miss Maurice set down in front of her. She looked around the kitchen, scratching one arm. The fixtures and paint and molding were more dated than most. There was a small open fireplace along one wall that had been adjusted for a gas appliance (the whole house was kept hot, but the kitchen especially hotter than Carmen could usually stand for very long), and the stove an old iron one converted from wood to coal, but wood could still be burned in it if wood was all you had. The ladies kept this stove going from first thing in the morning until they were ready to head to bed at night, and next to it was an oil-fueled range they used to boil water for tea and so on with a kettle that was boiling on it now.

Miss Maurice came in then. "Near forgot," she said, and went, turned the oil stove off, which went out with a whoosh of flame, and took the kettle and filled a large brown clay water bottle with it. She wrapped it in a thick piece of old blanket, and handed it to Carmen. It was the exact degree of heat she had been needing all day and hadn't known it. She leaned her abdomen into it.

"Stay put for one more hand, maybe two," Miss Maurice said to her. "I'm on a winning streak."

Thursday Evening: Bump Miss Susie

The three two-bit pieces Miss Maurice had finally won and handed over to Carmen lay heavy in the pocket of her skirt. They would come in handy in a little while, but right now she was standing by the drinking fountain in Union Square, looking up at her front windows, wondering. Mr. Morris must have already gone, and Donna and Lucille might be getting into trouble. Two days ago Donna had covered Lucille's face in lipstick and yesterday it still hadn't come off, but Carmen didn't have money for cold cream. Mr. Morris had gotten some lunch things from Hollins Market, but he hadn't eaten all of it when she'd left.

What she was wondering was whether she ought to go in first and make sure the girls still had something to eat. They could put themselves to bed.

She had put herself to bed often enough, sometimes too early, sometimes before the sun went down, and she'd lie awake for hours, wearing her little bloomers and the under-blouse that tied with a faded ribbon she'd twirl between the fingers of one hand, over and over, while she told herself stories, mostly about living where girls flocked over the streets in their boots and short dresses and the enormous bows in their bobbed hair. Or she would listen to adult noises coming from downstairs, or the back yard, or the next room. When she was ten, she had to go with her grandmother to the clothing factory where Carmella swept buttons and thread off the floor, and it was Carmen's job to pick out the threads and sort through the buttons by color. That was fun for an hour, tolerable for about another hour after that, and then it had crushed her, sitting alone on a stool with a big wooden box cutting into her knees, pushing the buttons into piles around the bottom of that box. Nowhere in her imagination had anybody ever had to do anything as crushing as that. The morning after the first day, she cried she didn't want to go, but her mother, who was lying in bed, looking for the umpteenth time at an old magazine full of illustrated white people that she kept next to her, had gotten up and given Carmen a shake and a good slap. "Don't you tell me what you don't want to do, girl," she said.

So after a while, she had gotten used to it, and often ended the long days amusing and comforting herself by climbing into the lap of whatever man had been at home when she got there, often too tired to eat anything, and putting her arms up around the man's neck. She'd say, "Hello, Daddy," to him just before falling asleep into his shirt. The middle of one night she had wakened to find the man on top of her, not penetrating but rubbing himself into her legs, she had opened her eyes wide and gasped, and he had laughed and said, "Why, hello, Baby!" She was frightened but she laughed right back up at him. What he was doing didn't hurt, in fact it didn't feel too bad, and when he was done he had wiped her off very gently and spent the rest of the night until she fell back to sleep again telling her stories of working on one of the big ships during the war, down in the hole, singing to her the song that he had sung to himself at sea, and she fell asleep humming it into his warm, sweet-smelling chest. Later there were others, and all of them hurt her but who her mother said she must let them be, but when she did, she would think of that man, and look up into the face of the rough one, wink, and chuckle, "Why, hello, Baby!" and then thought would disappear back into night, and often she wouldn't remember another thing.

Oh! That's right, she thought now, there were crackers and butter in the icebox, too. So that was all right, then. The girls had plenty. She turned and walked in the other direction, to a tavern she knew where the men were also plenty and the cigarettes went around well, and there might even be a shot or two of something that wasn't to drink. She clicked her heels, humming "Bump Miss Susie" as she walked.

Friday Night: You Get What You Get

Carmen opened the door and found Paddy Dolan there. He was filthy, and he smelled like the last day of the dead. She pinched her nose.

"Where in hell you been? What you want?" she asked him.

"Just shut up and let me in," he said. "I know your boyfriend ain't in there, I seen him leave."

"Well, he's coming back."

"Sure he is."

She spit in his face, and watched as he wiped the spit off with his broken hand, looking her straight in the eyes all the while.

She opened the door wider, and stepped back, and he went in. The landing was dark, and smelled sour and brown, like a nursing home, and all the doors were shut.

"Up here," Carmen said, and he followed her swaying backside up the stairs.

She woke up a few hours later to the sound of a record player needle being scratched over a record. Lucille was standing next to the long wooden console with her hand in the interior, apparently simply sliding the record player arm back and forth over the surface of a record, and she was staring at Carmen without blinking. There was a jelly stain on her undershirt and she was wearing some old pair of summer pajama bottoms that barely fit over her bottom and legs. Her hair was a mess of rats' nests, and her eyeglasses down low over her nose. Carmen was enraged at the sight of her.

"Goddamn you, you stupid little thing," she said, as she thought, under her breath, and tried to leap up from the sofa to smack her out of the room, but the sex and needle hangover she didn't know she had slammed her down again. She draped the back of one arm over her eyes.

The screeching kept on. "Goddamn it, Donna, Carmen, Lucille, whatever your name is, stop that goddamned racket before I go crazy." But this was said almost under her breath. And then the sound stopped, and then there was not another sound except for the toilet flushing and someone whistling. Carmen opened her eyes and Lucille was still standing there, looking at her, unblinking, her arm extended inside the console.

Four: Saturday Morning: Every Once in a While

Carmen stared at the empty, rusting can of spaghetti she had opened for the girls at dinner last night. They were still asleep and she had sat here at the table all night, the radio playing softly until it went off the air. She had listened to the buzzing for a while and then finally snapped it off altogether.

She had felt, after Paddy coming over, that she wanted to be just with her girls after all. When she was able to get up, she found him in the living room with them, and shooed him out. They sat on the couch, backs to the room, coloring up some newspaper. She'd felt a deep anger cut into her from somewhere. She didn't know what it was, she wanted to ignore it so it wouldn't spoil everything.

"Why, hello, Baby!" she cried out to them, a wide smile on her still deep red-lipsticked mouth. But they did not look up and smile and answer, "Hi, Mommy!" as they ought. They flinched, but they didn't turn or speak or look up from what they were doing. She wanted to beat them then, but in fact she didn't often have it in her to hit the girls when she wasn't loaded or hung over. She stood in the middle of the room, felt foolish, felt the rage begin to rise over that. She saw somebody's slipper laying on the floor, gave it a good kick, and it swirled across the floor and under the sofa.

"What do you want, spaghetti for dinner?" she asked them, and they said "Uh-huh" nearly in unison, but she was even too tired to smack them for their manners, even though that wasn't beating, that was being a mother.

As she pivoted toward the kitchen, the room seemed to move up and down in a wave. "Oh. No. Not again," she thought. She let out a kind of cry and put one hand on her abdomen, and at that the girls turned to see what the matter was, and then they did come running to her. They placed their small hands on her body, patting her back and her stomach, the top of Donna's head coming up to about her shoulder and Lucille's resting into her breast. She reached her own arms out and around them, and held them to her, and felt good again. She threw her head back and laughed.

"Well, girls," she'd said down into their heads in the soft and funny voice that they loved but hardly ever heard, "guess what? *Mr. Morris slept here.*"

"Mr. Morris slept here," she said to herself now at the table, out loud. She picked up the spaghetti can and threw it into the sink. One of the girls rustled and turned over, and began to snore lightly the way children do.

"Every goddamned body slept here," she said. "Everybody sleeps here."

Part Two: Young Mr. Emerson.

Thursday Morning: She's Like the Swallow

Young Mr. Emerson had already lived the life that everyone would be living ten years or so ahead. He had just celebrated his fiftieth birthday two days or weeks or so ago. He lived two doors down from Petie in the house his mother and father had raised him in, but now, excepting one cat, he had had the place to himself for almost four decades. Waking, he realized it was not remotely near ten, shut his eyes, determined that he would stay there in bed until he couldn't stand it anymore, and that time had better be closer to ten than not, or somebody was going to hear about it. He had never met her but knew who Carmen was, and wondered what she might be up to. *If she's up, she ain't been to bed yet*, he thought, and then whistled lightly for the cat to jump up and lay on his chest, which it did. Carmen fell out of his mind as routinely as she seemed to enter it. She was too young to ever have been one of his regulars, when he had regulars.

He lay for what felt like all day, all the while his eyes shut tight. The kitten had apparently found something to eat, it wasn't fussing at him to feed it. The motor of purring and its heat right under his chin weren't annoying enough to swat it away. He settled a bit deeper into the covers, and began to think about his mother.

Young Mr. Emerson's mother had been quite an accomplishment. She was very pretty, with soft light hair that was neither flaxen nor gold nor any kind of yellow, but also not simply brown, fawn, or any other word that he knew. His father, Big Mr. Emerson, used to sing to her, "I Dream of Jeannie with the Light Brown Hair," to which she'd reply, "Oh, Mister. My hair is not bloody brown." When Young declared one morning, around the age of five, in the interests of emulating her and of saying something with exactly the correct intention, that he was not interested in having any bloody eggs, she turned to him and sighed, and said, "Oh, Young. I guess you had better go get the belt."

He cried, and screamed, but she'd said nothing. She sat down opposite to him at the dining table, watching him, her elbows on the edge of the table, which he already knew one must not ever do if one were a well-mannered little boy, and pressed the tips of her fingers together below her nose, her eyebrows raised just slightly. He stopped howling, stared at her with bleak eyes, then slid down and went to get his father's thick brown belt, the one he only wore on Saturdays when he wore his awful slacks, the ones he got drunk in once a week when he would sit out on the back steps and drink tumbler after tumbler of something brown, something that made his breath smell sharp and sour, and made him shove his mother around and kiss her for what Young knew had to be far too long.

When Young returned with the belt, his mother held it for a moment, looking at him speculatively, then dealt him one blow across the face that split his lip and cut his eyelid. She neither ministered to these wounds nor spoke of them again. From that point on, when she told him to go get the belt, she might strike him with it, or she might take it from him, in the manner of accepting a plate of food or a dishrag she'd asked for, and hold on to it, stroking it, staring into space. Young would never know which she'd do, and by the time he was seven, he didn't feel anything about it. He knew that he must stand before her until she gave him leave to move, and this might not come for ten minutes, or half an hour, and that at the end of whatever time it had been, he was as likely to be hit as not. It was as if his presence meant nothing to her. Still, he figured out quickly that he was most in danger of the belt if he said a thing she judged he should not, and this he solved easily. He simply ceased to speak at all, other than to say, "Yes, ma'am," or "No, ma'am," but pronouncing each judiciously, so as not to convey the impression that he wished to be spiteful, or arrogant, or that he didn't know who he thought he was. He was sure who he thought he was, in any event.

She had died in time for Young's father not to have gone from being Big Emerson to Old Emerson, but she had never called him Big. Her last word in fact had been "Mister," spoken clearly from the small hospital bed in the ward where sixteen-year-old Young had been allowed to visit her. She had not had the influenza but something else that had come on quickly, but Big insisted should be treated for at the hospital. It was judged Mrs. Emerson was not going to live, and Big declared that whether he would catch 'flu by going to the hospital or not, Young was going to be there in the room with her at the end. They stood side by side at the foot of the bed, his mother's eyes on his father, she trying to say something, God only knew what, and all Young could think of was where he last left the big brown belt, which over the years had been kept though it had been some years since it was long enough to span his father's waist. Then she said it, "Mister," and she died with her eyes open, breathing out a long, slight breath.

Young's father didn't bother to call for a nurse or a doctor, but yanked Young by the elbow and said, "Come, boy, we're getting out of here." He gave Young his first hard drink then, at the first tavern they came to on Fayette Street, and they stayed a long time. They told the barman it was a family wake, and he took a drink with them in sympathy. Young had thrown up several times before Big realized he ought to get some food in the boy, but by then Young couldn't keep anything down, and at last they staggered home to find dishes still in the sink, sheets tousled on the beds, and his mother's pocketbook laying on the kitchen table.

Young had swayed on his feet, holding on to the back of a chair so as not to fall down on the floor. Big opened the bag, pulled out a handful of things, tossed them on the table, and out of this collection picked up and opened a coin purse, where he found only a few copper coins and a hairpin. He whistled between his teeth, then took the bag again and clenched the bottom of it. He grunted, turned the bag inside out, and tore at the silk lining of it with his teeth, which nearly made Young cry, as if he were watching his father take his teeth to his mother's very flesh. But then Big was proved to be right, for paper cash came out of the slit in the silk like a caesarian birth, more than one hundred dollars, and Big set them on the table as if they had been holy cards and he a convert or a grandmother. He looked at them with affection, too, Young saw, and then he dug deep into his own pockets, where he always kept every piece of money he had. He planted these right next to Mrs. Emerson's newborn cash, and sat down and appeared to think.

"I don't know how she done this," he said finally, "but it's a good thing all around she was smart." He looked up at Young, and said with pride and something proprietary that later Young would know emanated from love and desire, both as alive as they must have been the day he first saw her and the afternoon they had wed.

"It's the reason I married her. She was pretty, but the pretty girls flocked round me like bees in them days. She was the smart one."

Young had also not said a word to his father since he was seven years old, letting his yes's and no's to his mother stand in for all the conversation he could muster with either of them, but now he said, "Oh," and his father nodded as if they'd been speaking to and understanding each other all along, as if Big the man and Young the boy were bound by an honorable understanding of self that was perfect, and that this made everything all right, which Young felt that it did.

Big picked up two gold dollars and several pieces of the paper, along with a few pennies and the hairpin.

"I'm going to leave you with all this," he said, pointing to what remained on the table. "Tomorrow, take the streetcar down to the bank, and have the banker change one of these"—he picked up one of the bills—"into coins and change. When you run out, go back down and do the same thing. Don't spend the gold coins until you have to. When you run out all the way, it'll be time to get a job. Nobody from the police or the schools will come looking for you here. Don't drink at home, and don't ever bring a girl here. Thomas over on Pratt will help you get the right things to eat, and Barry down the road won't let you get too drunk. When you're seventeen, tell Pauline I sent you."

He then thrust his hand out, and Young took it, and he said, "Goodbye. I'll see you again, God willing."

And then he was gone, and Young knew that he was going to be happier than he had ever been in his life.

Shabbat Shalom

Young Mr. Emerson discovered that he enjoyed cleaning and washing up for himself, and when he had asked, Thomas, who owned the little dry-grocer's in the next block, called his wife out to the counter, and she told him how to order milk from the milk wagon, and ice, and how to haggle for vegetables when the colored men came around leading their mule-drawn wagons. She told him which dry goods he should keep on hand, and which it was better to come up to their place for every once in a while, and she told him what to use in the event, heaven forbid, he should find himself connected to a dirty girl. Thomas told him not to smoke at home, but would sell him a cigarillo that he could smoke by parts at the tavern.

He hadn't gone out to the tavern right away, mostly because he was worried how drinking would deplete his money. He found, though, that one of those changed bills would get him through an entire week or two of spending his money on damned well anything he could think of to spend it on, and that he could drink quite a bit on one coin, and soon he was at the tavern three and four nights out of the week. No one mentioned his youth, no one seemed to notice, or if they did, perhaps they thought this was the best way for an orphan who was nearly a grown man to settle his affairs. If he needed a new collar or shoelaces or tooth powder from Woolworth's, he'd take a bill, and they would change it for him just as if he'd gone to the bank, and that would save him a trolley ride downtown. He'd seen Pauline, and he thought he'd like to turn seventeen just as soon as the opportunity presented itself.

It had one day, and he had promptly fallen in love and asked to marry her despite the difference in their ages. When she'd laughed at him he hadn't minded, but pulled her over to him again and said, "No hard feelings?" and that was possibly the first time in his life he'd made a joke to someone else at his own expense. He did run out of money eventually, but kept all of the gold coins in a cigar box as a memento of his mother, who now had you asked him was the embodiment of the glories of the saints Elizabeth and Ann and even the Blessed Mother. He found a job that might turn into something, running errands first for the Western Union, and then selling papers for the *News American*, where he found luck covering funerals and writing obituaries, eventually famed on the floor for the particular elegance and lack of sentimentality in his elegiac style. He had been too young for the first war, and was too old for the second. He had been happy, and productive, and had courted not a few very nice women, at least four of whom would have been very glad to marry him, but he never put the question to them.

And then, on what would become the last day of the second Great War, he had woken up, tried to get out of bed, and found he could not. He had been reading the reports that were coming in from Europe and Asia, and what he read there he identified with in some curiously personal way, although he despised Jews and colored people and had never previously had any reason to change his mind about them, never having come in their way other than to buy things off the nigger carts or have his shoes shined or his hair oiled in the men's room. When he had come across one photograph of a little boy in Berlin, with a yellow star on his knitted vest sweater and a large bandage on his forehead, Young felt a deep sense of injustice in his heart and soul, more real than anything he had felt since he was small and had stopped talking, and was sick nearly to the point of expelling his dinner onto the archives room floor.

He stayed in bed all that day, despite hunger and needing the toilet. He slept, woke, daydreamed about who knew what, slept again. It wasn't until he knew that he had to get a drink and that there was none in the house that he forced himself to roll off the bed. From there, he crawled to the dresser and extracted some socks, and stood, staggered to the bathroom, used the toilet, and spit blood into the basin. He looked at himself, as if from a great distance, he thought, as if the entire world had gone quiet and blank. It was novel, and he realized in some part of himself that he enjoyed the feeling.

This had been a Saturday, and normally he worked a half-day Saturdays. On Sunday he felt fine, got up, left the house, and decided he'd just go on "a nice long walk." He walked down Lombard Street for blocks, enjoying himself hugely, but still bothered with the sense that his physical body was far away from the rest of the corporeal universe, and then he was downtown, near the water, and still he kept walking. "Maybe I'll walk all the way to the East Side," he thought, "and get something to eat or something."

Not a Desecration

He reached Lloyd Street, saw a man in a frock hat and long hair coming towards him on Lombard, and realized he wished to speak to him — he didn't know the man, he simply he wanted to talk to someone, he had kept silent too long all day. But the man, deep in thought, didn't notice Young, and turned up Lloyd, crossing the street to Young's side as he did. Without thinking, Young followed him, a slight, rather short man with harsh features that in some way reminded Young of Big Emerson. They reached a square building that looked like a church and yet did not, and the man began to ascend the stairs. Young waited for him to open the door, but it appeared that the man had only wanted to reassure himself the door was locked. He turned, and saw Young standing there.

"What do you wish, please?" the man said in a heavily accented voice. He seemed nervous, as if perhaps he worried Young wished ill for him or even intended to rob or strike him.

"Oh. I thought I might like to go inside, you know, to pray." Young hadn't said a sincere prayer in twenty years.

"But it's Sunday."

"I know." What was the matter with that? "But, you know, waking and sleeping, on the doors and all." He remembered this from his mother.

The man smiled suddenly and then looked keen.

"Are you?" he asked with a friendly but intense look about his eyes.

"Am I what?" Young answered, and immediately the smile changed to an efficient grimace.

"Oh. Pardon me. No matter. Thank you for your interest, but we are not open today."

Some kind of Amish, Young bet. He had read about the Amish in a file at the paper, and knew they had odd habits of worship, and he'd remembered about the hats and the long hair and beards, although this man wore a moustache. Still, the file indicated one might encounter Amish of several different stripes, and why not here in Baltimore, which was not very far from Pennsylvania. Perhaps this was a mission or some kind of business enterprise. It was interesting.

At that moment, a young man came out of a house opposite, and as God was Young's witness, it was the boy of the Berlin photograph, or someone just like him. He had on a sleeveless knitted argyle vest, and a long scar over his right eye. And there was a yellow star sewn to the sweater.

Young stared as if looking at himself in a photograph. He rocked on his heels, put his hand out, and the bearded man hastened down the stairs and took hold of his elbow to steady him. The young man across the street saw them, turned, hurried back into his house.

"*Tschah, tschah*," the man said. "It's all right. He wears it in memory only. He does not wear it in public. It is not a desecration."

Young stared at the man. Not Amish, Jewish. One of those people from that place: of course, he had seen photographs of them.

"I have been there, too," he found himself saying. "I have seen a boy like that one. I thought it was that boy."

He meant only the photograph, he was not intending to lie outright, but the other man stopped where he stood and stayed quiet a long time, holding Young's elbow lightly enough but so that he should not fall down. The grasp felt like a thing that

Young had not known touch could feel like, as if it comprehended him, and as if speech, Young's tormentor and betrayer, would never be needed again.

But then the man did speak, hoarsely. "And you are not. Yet you have seen."

He seemed to have no other words. He began to say what Young had to imagine were prayers in some Jewish language, and at once he felt terribly sick, and angry, and disgusted at the feel of the man's hand on his elbow.

These sentiments must have moved across his face, for the man dropped his hand away, and he said, "I beg you to forgive me. May you live a long time, and may you speak to those who have not seen. *Shalom.*"

Young felt as if he had entered a brothel and found only men and children selling themselves inside. But from that moment, his every spare moment was spent in the newspaper archives, or writing, or drinking, and when he was not doing these things, he was at the Enoch Pratt Free Library downtown. He found out everything about being Jewish he could learn without asking anyone directly, memorized whole passages of Hillel and such portions of Mishnah as he could find translated and reasonably understandable, and began to dot his conversation with Yiddishisms he heard from comedians on the radio.

He also began to attend the services at the synagogue, silently praying the Rosary in Latin to himself when the congregation or the rabbi began to speak in Hebrew. He found the singing of the cantor unutterably uplifting, and would hum those melodies he could recall to himself as he stood ironing his clothing or frying scrapple in the pan, always ending with, "Queen of the Heavens, Queen of the May," and nodding toward the sky.

He would later refer to this time as his Second Period of Happiness. He was noticed at the synagogue but never introduced himself. Still, he knew his unconscious, still fallacious admission to the man of the steps had spread, for he was treated by some of the members with deference punctuated by a kind of terror and, he thought, disgust, as if they had to admit to themselves that this thing had happened to themselves. By others he felt as if he were bound to them in blood, and that to speak of what was between them would be to rend the fabric of heaven into tatters even worse than those in which it now found itself.

He found the silence of the people exhilarating, the solitude exactly what suited him, the stares of these strangers he eventually began to label as "Four Eyes," "Jewest of the Jew Beaks," "Massive Bosom," and "Yellow Teeth," the most blessed and perfect form of communication he had ever experienced. At work he had taken to not talking at all, and his obituaries had become the templates around which lesser men at other newspapers fashioned their own scribblings in despair.

The first day he walked into shul, he had been kindly asked to sit at the back of the room, but not to leave, and eventually his rocking and humming—though he never mastered Hebrew or knew the sense of many of the words—had a perfection of cadence that misled children and strangers. He never sought to ingratiate himself personally into the congregation, was never invited to a meal, was never stopped outside services to share a smoke or a bit of talk. He would leave proudly, trot down the steps as if exiting a beloved alma mater, and walk squarely away down the couple of miles to the corner of Lombard and Stricker, turn right, and sigh as he entered his house.

Thursday Afternoon: You Remember the Kind of Thing

Young never went outside until the sun began to go down, he lived on what the milkman and the bread truck could deliver by day, and he drank by night, nearly never walking up to what had become Dolan's grocery. He paid his expenses out of a pension from the *News American,* where he had remained until his left arm had been badly disfigured in an accident two years ago, and because he'd been smart and signed for a settlement, they sent him ten dollars a week, and that was plenty for him, barring a stretch to get through Sundays. He followed his father's advice and did not drink or smoke in the house, and he would not go to the taverns on Sundays, so those were bad days. He had a feeling that if he could account for his Sundays, he would not be very pleased with himself, but this was a Thursday, and Thursdays were goddamn great.

His father, who had not returned and who Young supposed must have passed on a good while back, was someone Young thought about a lot. He wondered what his father would have made of what Young now called "all that Jew nonsense," and he thought about this nearly every day. The end of his time at the synagogue had eventually come, of course. A new man had come on to the newspaper in '47 or '48, Young couldn't quite remember now, and they'd met and talked about this and that over the course of the man's first week, but on Saturday he saw him again as they were leaving the morning service. The man, Martin had been the name, Young thought, raised his eyebrows but didn't otherwise acknowledge Young's presence, and he didn't say anything to him at work the next week. Young didn't think much of it, but the following Saturday a group of four men stood in the vestibule at the back of the synagogue, and as he entered they approached him.

None of the men seemed very willing to meet his eyes. They stood before him silently for so many moments that Young began to think that one of them might strike him. Finally, the one that Young had named "Young Mr. Shamir" spoke up.

"There is a difficulty," he began, but at the words Young took a step back, held up one palm as if to stop them all from approaching, though they had not moved. They did not speak, the expressions on their faces showing differing degrees of grief and disappointment. He knew there was nothing to say. He turned, walked down the steps, never went back.

From that moment—and he held no grudge over this with Martin, with whom he'd become rather good pals at the paper— his spiritual life such as it had been was effectively over. His obituaries became so pedestrian that he was finally taken off them and relegated to fact-checker. His schooling, as it had been largely self-directed, seemed to fade overnight, and he began to speak in the slovenly way that characterized him now. He eschewed all women, and the company of most men, and settled down into the drink.

And then the accident to his arm had happened, through nobody's fault, nobody's carelessness or drunkenness, and he was at home, with his cat, and his daily round.

Friday Afternoon: Routine Matters

Twilight, now, that was his favorite time of day, and it would be twilight soon, but not yet. Just now it was about three o'clock and he was leaning slightly out of his bedroom window, looking up and down Stricker Street, spitting down on to the walk, timing how long it took the spit to land, trying to get each lob to land in the exact same place, like horseshoes. He heard a screen open slowly in its frame, looked toward the sound, saw the young girl, Catherine, whom he always called Connie because he could never keep anyone's name straight, getting home, fumbling with the front door key. *Connie*, he thought as he always did. *She's going to grow up to be a little something.*

"Nah, she won't," he said aloud. "Not if she keeps wearin them saddle shoes like at."

He shut up. He could not stand the sound of his own voice.

The painted china clock on the bedroom mantelpiece chimed out four times. Young got up, bending his head a little under the window sash, stretched, walked over to the clock, turned the key in the round brass hole, and wound exactly four and a half times around. The clock began to tick more brightly. He replaced the clock, stretched again, looked around the room. *Think I'll take me a bath*, he thought. *Then I'll read the paper some.*

He lowered his soaped and scrubbed and dried and boxer-short clad haunches into the relative inflexibility of his living room lounge chair. He didn't know why, or if, it was really called a lounge chair, but it was old, upholstered in a brown velvet material that looked like horse hair and might have been. The carvings on its frame, a painted brown wood of some kind, were round, ornately dug into roses and other images of no particular identity, and he still meant to get the few smears of paint off the upholstery where whoever had done the painting had been careless, but that was a difficulty, because whom after the sun went down could he ask a question about how he would go about doing such a thing? He didn't know how to do it, how to get the paint off, and when he had asked at the tavern, they'd just looked at him like he was crazy. They had looked at him, though, so he knew he had opened his mouth, but possibly the words he'd thought he had said were not the ones that actually came out. Or perhaps he didn't speak loud enough for other people to hear. But nobody had said that. Maybe they were just surprised he'd said anything at all.

Anyways, he said to himself. If he had a telephone he could call the hardware store. The lounge chair was not long enough to lie down in (*If I lay down in it I have to bend my knees*, he said to himself or out loud as he prepared to get into it, as if that meant something) but the length of it fit the entirety of his legs stretched out, for he had not grown into a tall man like his father.

This fully stretching out his legs upon a piece of living room furniture was a luxury he reserved as a pleasure in a day filled with long hours and small pleasures, and he straightened his bow tie at the collar, adjusted the fabric of his boxer shorts above his knees, and then began to cry, enjoying the crying in the same way that, each morning he managed to get out of bed while it was still morning, after he had finished his eggs and bacon, he enjoyed a nice long laugh, and each noon he enjoyed the twenty-seven push-ups he did on the earth floor of his cellar, wearing nothing but his undershorts and sleeveless undershirt, listening to the rhythm of the ringer washer cleanse his spare dress shirt and pair of slacks. He had two of each, and whichever was in the laundry he called his spare.

His feet hurt him. He looked down at his ankles, blue and red with clustered veins and broken capillaries, admiring them. By the end of the evening they would be round and puffy, but now they were nearly sleek, the elegant bones visible and not precisely sharp. Elegant, he thought, elegant and intelligent. Where was that from? A beer slogan? Laundry soap? Ladies' face powder? *Hmm*, he thought. *Maybe I made it up.*

"I am elegant and intelligent," he said out loud. By nine o'clock he'd be telling this to Pauline, the name he had given to the tree in his back yard, just before he unzipped his fly and pissed all over her trunk, but now he was pleased with the thought, and believed it, because indeed his ankles were admirable, extending out past the cuffs of his spare pair of slacks. He crossed them, and heard the cat cry from somewhere in the house. *I didn't get no milk out for it yet. I'ma half to do that before long.*

The cat cried again. *Quit cryin.* It cried again. "You stop that or I'll give you something to cry for," he called out, but this iteration merely produced more of the same. Young Emerson took a last wistful look at his ankles, uncrossed and swung them over the edge of the lounge chair, and hoisted himself up. Christ knew he couldn't sit there and listen to that cat crying for the next two hours.

Saturday, Two A.M.: Not a Big Eater

Young Mr. Emerson wanted a glass of milk. But there was no milk. He wanted an egg, and some toast and butter, and some bacon. He knew he had a day-old dry onion roll, and a can of some kind of soup or other and that there was some cat food. He thought he might have a little bit of cheese in the icebox, and he knew there was a block of lard. Maybe there was some tea. He was hungry, but he wanted milk and bread, and there wasn't any.

It was some awful hour, he thought. The bread truck would not stop today because he had omitted to put in a new order last night, and he couldn't get out of bed and make out a new slip and open the door this morning to catch the truck before it came by, although that wouldn't even happen for another hour or two at least. Yesterday morning he had still had some milk and butter and eggs, but he'd eaten and drunk it all, and then last night as he staggered up the steps and seen the milk bottles there with no slip in the box to indicate what he wanted today, he had sublimely refused to make one out and put it in.

He'd gotten drunk, drunk-drunk, and over the course of the drunk had decided he was never going to eat again, and this, he would have told you what, felt like the best thing that had ever happened in the entire course of his existence. He was not a big eater anyway. That was true. It was also true that the more he drank, the less he felt like eating, but last night, last night he had arrived at the certitude that eating was somehow wrong, even defective, that no one should eat anymore, and that the state of euphoria in which he found himself would last indefinitely, just as he inevitably thought that the state of drunkenness would last forever when he was in it, and that the wish for food would from this moment forward would no longer trouble him.

Even on the way home, when he had turned into an alley to vomit, that had felt good and right, too, and had not produced any hunger, but a kind of magical emptiness that appeared to him to be even better than what he'd felt sitting on the bar stool with the last of who knew how many shot glasses of the night in his hand. He had arrived back at his front door and spurned the milk bottle crate at ten p.m., fallen violently into bed and immediately to sleep, and just past midnight had just as violently wakened so hungry and empty that he thought that all he ever wanted to do again in life was eat, and eat.

But now he couldn't force himself out of bed to see if that cheese might still be in the icebox, nor to fill out an order from the milkman that would include milk, and bread, and eggs. Why was that again? There was a problem with this, and it had come and gone in his mind a couple of times now.

Oh, yes, this was it: Because what would be the good of eggs without bacon? He could not fry an egg in lard, nor in butter. He couldn't bear the taste of it. And he didn't know how else to make an egg. And then what would the point of the bread be? And he was double-goddamned if he was going to make toast and dip it into a goddamned glass of milk.

"God god damn it," he said out loud.

However, he thought as his stomach growled, Dolan's would open by eight, and they would have bacon. He could get up and put on his robe and slippers, go down the front stairs very quietly, tiptoe to the kitchen and eat the cheese right now, and then slowly step back to the living room, fill out the slip, silently open the door—no, that wouldn't work. He had allowed himself to be fooled into purchasing one of those new aluminum screen doors with the mechanism that didn't slam, and that had seemed like a superlative idea at the time, but he later and to his deep chagrin had realized the air-pump noise of the goddamned thing would alert damn near every waking and sleeping person in likely a three-block radius every time he opened it, and while he was comforted by the thought that if anybody else were to open it, he would hear them—and by the clock, he'd know if it was the mailman opening up the door to put the mail in the slot, or the newspaper boy setting the *News American* in the vestibule—

All right, he could slip out the back door, walk down the alley and up the block to the front steps, put the slip into the crate, walk up the block and around—no. That wouldn't work, either. He'd have the cheese eaten, but that man across the street who worked on the B&O would be up and he'd look out and see him.

Christ. All right. Here's what he'd do. He'd go into the bathroom, run a tub of water like that jackass Nevan Dolan had done—it was all anybody who could talk was talking about last night at the tavern—and wait for a heart attack to kill him and if that didn't work, he'd put his straight razor next to him on the bathtub ledge and slice his wrists open and then that would take care of everything.

Okay. That's what he'd do, and that would be fine—oh, and he'd be sure to shut the bathroom door so the cat wouldn't get upset or eat anything he shouldn't. Somebody would come for the cat eventually. It was a loud damn cat.

He flung himself out of bed, not bothering with robe or slippers, barreled out of the bedroom and lurched down through the length of the house to the bathroom. He weaved a little, the soles of his feet cold on the floor, and leaned over the toilet bowl and threw up another time.

He stood up.

He was so hungry he couldn't think. He wasn't going to kill himself, he was going to eat, and he didn't care if it was lard or a chunk of ice or a dry teabag. He ran as well as a drunk man can run down the back stairs to the kitchen, threw open the icebox door, and saw what he'd completely forgotten about, the end of a ham he had been keeping to make soup. The brown rind covered mostly fat but a little bit of flesh, and he could taste the salt of it right there in his mouth. He pulled it out with the block of lard and threw them both down on the counter top next to the sink, pulled out the big carving knife, and began to cut into the ham. The first bite was half-fat, cold, thick, and soft, with a greasy aftertaste that turned his stomach. *Treyf*, some deceased place in his mind said, to which he answered, *Shut up, you bastard. I eat what I please.*

The ham was not going to be enough. He saw the bag that held the onion roll on top of the icebox, took it out and tried a bite, but it was so stale he could barely manage to rip off a mouthful, and the hard crust scraped the inside of his cheek and his tongue.

The slip, he said to himself, *just fill out the slip. It doesn't matter. Just fill it out.*

But he wouldn't open that front door, he knew that. He could go around out back, though, he thought, if he did it right now, if he checked off the boxes on the slip, put on his overcoat and his shoes, and went out the back very quietly. He could do that, surely he could.

The alley smelled of old water sitting, lichen growing on the small stones of the cement, cold brick, and tar. This, what the out-of-doors smelled like, he barely noted, but he watched for rats and garbage cans so as not to run into either. The rear of the funeral home took up most of what would be its yard, and he stepped out from the back corner of that building out onto Pratt Street, under a street light. He clutched the milk order slip tighter in his hand, pulled his overcoat around him like a bathrobe, and walked gently up the half-block, turned and in less than a minute was in front of his house. He looked up and down the street, saw not a light on nor a shade up, laughed to himself in quiet triumph, and tucked the order slip into the wooden crate, between two milk bottles. He'd even ordered cream this time, and an extra dozen of eggs, and another loaf of bread. Just the thought of the food filled him up, and he knew he could survive until the truck came by.

Saturday Morning: All Right, Steve

As he turned to retrace his steps to the alley, he nearly jumped out of his skin at the sight of a small man coming up to him, slowly, and in fact he was not at all certain at first that he was not seeing a ghost. But the man's footsteps made sound, and the man himself seemed to be breathing hard and heavily as if the act of breathing was cutting into some part of him, and that Young could hear the cutting, not of flesh but of bone or, going by the insides of a chicken, of the thick cartilage that separated the lungs from the chest. Then Young saw that it was not a man, but a boy, that cat-swinging boy who beat his dog and who thought he was in love with that foolish girl, Connie. Young always called him Steve, but he knew that wasn't his name.

The boy came right up to him and stopped. He didn't seem to want to do anything else. Young waited.

"I need to get me to the B&O," the boy said in a whisper.

Young didn't say anything.

"I need to get there," he said again. He was forcing the words out, and sounded like he might be crying. "I can't make it."

And then he had to pause and breathe some more, and then he said a word that Young immediately knew was not a word he often said, maybe not one that he ever said.

"Please."

Not *Help me*, but *Please*, and hearing that Young would help him any way that he could, and he had not known that before, either.

"Okay, Steve," he said.

Young Mr. Emerson took a deep breath, and despite his frailty grabbed Petie, whose name the boy's really was, by the hand and dragged him into his house through the front door, "For I am damned if I shall walk through the tracks of the Baltimore and Ohio Railroad without socks on," he said. He was no longer hungry and he didn't care who might be watching. He forced Petie into a chair in the living room, where the cat immediately jumped on Petie's lap and he began to stroke it with one finger as he stared out into the middle of the floor, and wept it seemed only because he could not help it.

"I'll be just a minute," Young said to him when he saw this, but when Petie didn't respond he put out his hands as if to embrace him, but didn't touch him, then straightened himself again. "I'll be right back," he said, paused, turned, and went upstairs.

He dressed in his Sunday clothes, including a bow tie, but moved quickly and didn't take a bit longer than putting on his everyday things would have done. He pulled on dress stockings, with garters to finish, then his shoes, then put his overcoat back on over everything, tapped his way back downstairs, got his hat from the cupboard, and entered the living room, finding Petie as he'd left him.

"All right then!" Young said brightly, as if Petie were his own son and they were meeting again after many years, and it was his job to figure out what they were going to do and talk about. "Let us essay the historical haunts of the rail yard," he said what he hoped was gaily, and it came to him that he was speaking as he used to do, back at the newspaper, like an educated man, a man who had a life of interest with significance to spare. This frightened him, but he didn't know why, but nor did he care to stop.

Petie didn't move, and it came to Young that possibly he couldn't, so he took the boy by one hand, extended his other arm around his back, and lifted him as gently as he could.

"Aaaah," Petie cried, and the sound of it nearly broke Young's heart.

"I'm sorry, boy," he said. "Do you not want to go? We don't have to go. I can get you home if you want."

"Please," Petie said again, and Young knew that he did not mean that he wanted to go home.

"All right!" Young said again brightly and far too loudly. "We're off to the races, then. Come along, now," and he steered Petie through the three doors, banging his own body through the screen door, not hearing the pump as it wheezed the screen shut behind them.

They took the three steps to the pavement, turned, and, step by excruciating step, Young holding Petie like a dance partner, his good arm still around the boy's waist, his poor hand lightly holding the boy's hand, they shuffled down the block.

They did not speak another word the entire forty-five minutes, as Young estimated, that it took them to walk the half dozen blocks to the B&O. The sun still not yet up, they had not encountered a soul on the street, nor a single vehicle other than a taxi that slowed to indicate a question to which Young waved the negative with his head. Petie's steps were as labored as those of a very old man, his breath thick and sharp, stepping down off of and up on to the curbs taking every bit of attention he had. Still, Young could tell his thoughts were far away, that he possibly had to force himself to continue to occupy his physical body, and what it had cost him to get to Young's front steps from wherever he had come from Young could scarcely bring himself to imagine.

He saw as they entered the rail yard that Petie was sort of pointing in the direction of one of the long buildings, and that there was a light on in what must have been the back room.

"All right, Steve," Young said aloud, shifted their direction, and made his way towards it.

Young stood in the fresh air on the small porch of the train caboose, watching the city melt away backwards. He had never in his life felt any better. Going somewhere. Had he still been a cigar-smoking man, he would have been smoking a cigar, despite the hour of the day. He wished for an ascot to wear around his throat, but felt that the bow tie was sufficiently dapper and nothing to be ashamed of.

They had met up with a man named Teddy (for the Real Roosevelt, he had said) with whom Petie seemed to be on excellent terms, and who, when he saw Petie, vowed terrible and profane vengeance on whoever had done those things to him, but Petie wouldn't give up the name. At the sight of coffee and sweet rolls on the table Young had just about passed out, but Teddy was not at all behind-hand in offering both all around, and so he had eaten to the full, and there had also been milk, and Teddy didn't seem to think that it was unmasculine or out of place in the slightest when Young asked if he could have a cupful. "Please, sir," he had replied, in fact. A little bit later, while they were giving Petie something to eat by the spoonful that seemed to be doing him some good, there were fried eggs and bacon and toast, and Young ate until he just about did pass out.

He loved these people, he decided. Why had he not ever met them before? He loved Teddy, completely. He liked this train, the motion of it, the sense of the world going in reverse order behind you as you forged ahead into the place where no one could walk backward anymore. He had no idea where they were going, or why, but he surely liked being here, and he was so happy.

He turned to check on Petie where he sat inside the caboose, propped up on a small chair and sitting on top of some cushions, looking still blankly out of the window. He hadn't cried when they'd gotten him up and onto the train, but there were some tears on his face now. A coal fire burned next to him in a small cast-iron stove, and every moment or so he would suck on the corner of a saltine cracker and lean over to the little table and try to lift the small cup of fruit juice Teddy had left there for him. Otherwise, Young thought that, had he not had his arm around him for all that while, he would have thought he could pass his hand completely through Petie's body and not have disturbed either one of them.

He turned back to the view. It was impressive, what you saw from the rail lines, he thought. Downtown they had passed first, and then there were houses, and more houses, a couple of trains in the opposite direction, and now they were headed into the countryside, where Young had never been. The sheer numbers of trees, mostly bare of anything but a few buds on a few of them, frightened him a little bit, and made him feel colder than he was. The morning light on them was beautiful, though, he thought, and he would like to draw how the light looked, or even to paint a picture of it with some real paints. He had some cans of house paints at home, but maybe he could make it to Woolworth's and they might have some real painter ones. Maybe he could get some of those.

And then the train started to slow, Young lurched slightly where he stood and he turned around. Teddy passed through the little door, nodded to Young.

"This is where he wants off, just about."

Petie raised his eyes then, and said, "I need to go down the beach. Not right there, though. Pretty close."

"Well, we'll get you as close as we can, boy. What you going to do? You want to come back today?"

Petie didn't answer. Young had no idea what to say, but then Teddy asked him directly, "You want to keep going? You can ride all day if you want to."

The temptation was intense, but Young had been asked by Petie to get him where he needed to be, and he wasn't there yet, and so he would stay with him, and he said so. "I better."

"All right, suit yourself," Teddy said cheerfully, and the train came to a full stop. "Let's get eem down, I don't know how, tell you the truth. I bet you going up was going to be a lot easier," and it proved to be. As soon as they were clear of the car and off the tracks, Teddy handed Young a thermos and paper bag full of something, and said, "Ima be back around eleven tonight, I'll look for you. Otherwise you can hop one tomorrow."

Young nodded, holding the bag in his teeth and the thermos in the crook of his bad arm, his good one once again around Petie's waist. Petie seemed to be doing a little bit better than before, he thought, for as the train pulled slowly out, Teddy waving to them before disappearing back into the car, Petie lifted his head and said, "Thank you."

Saturday Afternoon: Found and Lost

And as much as Young had enjoyed the train ride, he knew he had never been in so beautiful and wonderful a place as this small stretch of lake shore where Petie led him, though it again took them the better part of an hour to get down there. The water was muddy-colored under the overcast sky, but Young didn't mind this at all. It was still water, lapping softly at the bank in a way that made him think of a baby's cradle rocking, and that perhaps he and Petie were the baby, safe and cared for. The openness and quiet made him a bit nervous, but he was willing to take the feeling.

Petie he propped against the trunk of a thin tree, using his overcoat as a cushion, and in his shirt sleeves in the shade Young was quite chilly. He had sniffed in the thermos and smelled coffee, and tasted it, and it had milk and sugar, too. How could it be that he had never met anyone like Teddy before, so kind, and so thoughtful yet straightforward a person? How had he never met anyone before who didn't seem to have some kind of terrible trouble that marked his days and distorted everything that he said and thought and did?

He would have to think about this later. There had been too many novelties in one day. After giving Petie a little of the coffee, which he kept down, and another couple of crackers, Young took off his shoes and socks, rolled up his slacks to the knee, and waded out into the cold water until he hit a patch of sun. He let it warm his body as he waited for his legs to do the same to the lake water. All Petie seemed to be able to do was sleep, though Young had gotten a good bit of the coffee into him, along with the end of a sweet roll from the paper bag. The rest was cold chicken and bread and butter, which, when Petie had shaken his head at it, Young had wolfed down until there was nothing left over. He was so used to spending the day doing very little that this much activity had worn him down, and now he was feeling something like irritation, and he wanted to sleep. He was cold, shivering, and Petie was shivering, too, every now and again. Young thought they would have to get out of there soon, but when he tried to say so to Petie, the boy's eyes filled, and he said once again, "Please."

So Young let it go, sat down at the water's edge in a small patch of sun, crossed his legs and closed his eyes. Soon he was standing at his kitchen table, counting out a dollar in coins to give to Pauline. His mouth and nose were nuzzled under one of her breasts, one arm around her waist, the other under her bottom, his body between her legs. He was walking to shul, fingering a rosary in his pocket, walking up on his toes, nodding to a stack of *News Americans* bundled in packing string on a corner. He rubbed the outside of his arm where his mother struck it with the belt, he pushed his dad upstairs and sang, "She's Like the Swallow," with him at the tops of their lungs. He sat in The

Bright Side tavern and had a fourth whiskey, he was immobilized before a stack of photographs in the newspaper archive room, he bowed with pleasure as the obit staff applauded his tribute to Franklin Delano Roosevelt. He was pulling the cat off his under-shirt, he was running a bath, listening to the water now running, now lapping like a lake, now hearing the sound of someone say-ing, "Hello."

"Hello!" the someone said again, and it was now, the lake, his eyes were open, and just off the shore a boy and a girl in a row boat, the boy rowing straight for him, the girl fair and nearly see-through in the bow turned toward him, the boy pale and dark, both smiling.

"Go on, get out of here!" he thought he yelled at them, but apparently nothing solid had come out of his mouth, for they kept smiling, and approaching, and finally there was nothing left to do but wade out into the water and pull the boat to shore. The girl tumbled out of it, into Young's arms and out of them, and he heard her say "Peter," in an under-voice so passionate that it thrilled and terrified him at the same time, and he knew that whatever it had been that he'd won today, it might well in that moment have been lost to him again.

Saturday Night: And In the End

Young Mr. Emerson woke up on the ground in the dark to the sound of the lake water lapping, himself damp and nearly dead with cold and very hungry again. There was no food or coffee left. He knew he had better get up and get moving or he would die of the cold. He remembered exactly where he was, and that he needed to get to the train tracks. He put his hand out for his shoes, put them on in the dark, and, after a couple of mishaps and small twig branches stinging into his face, he found his way to the tracks.

There was no street light, but there was a moon that was just about full, all but a small slice of it on the side, and he could see to get up on the tracks, to walk them, and then, for he was not a person whose physical instincts ever alerted him to anything, he was surprised to realize that he was not alone on the tracks, that something was behind him, something Petie had he been there could have told him was that sonofabitching mongrel Batista, who barked once as Young paused where he walked.

He did not turn around, nor pretend to, nor wish to. He had the same fear of dogs that he had of most other living creatures that were not human or house cat — he was nervous around those, but not afraid of most of them. He could handle as many people as he needed, and he only had the one cat, but dogs were another thing. He thought if he continued to hop along the tracks, one of two things would happen: he would come to some place where he could call out for help, wherever that might be, or the dog would overtake him and kill him, but either way, standing still was stupid. Then the dog's single bark, a command if he had ever heard one, told him he was right. In the moonlight, Young appeared like an old-fashioned cut-out silhouette, hopping like a woman with one shoe on over the tracks, a pony-sized animal picking its way over the tracks behind him.

But Teddy remembered his promise, and at last Young saw the train approach and slow at the crossing where he stood, the dog having abandoned him at some juncture or other, Young waving his arms madly in delight. They got him on to the caboose where, to his dismay, that part of the universe he had previously imagined could only be experienced in forward motion melted away in reverse, just as the streets and avenues and buildings down home had done, so that now he could not make sense of either. He was certain, holding on to the iron rail of the car porch and looking out into the night and the light of the moon, that had there been any other way to get home short of walking thirty miles over the course of the next three days and sleeping next to alley cans in the nights, he would have taken it.

He was reversing in himself as well, the solidified part of him that had been liquefied on the trip up to the lake that had changed him into a state wholly unfamiliar but completely welcome, not free but even independent of freedom, on which he had been changed from flesh to liquid perhaps even in the water of Lake Roland as he stood in it and hadn't known it was happening to him even as he was becoming part of the same substance with it, now with each mile and marker and train track clicked away again behind him, began to turn Young back again slowly more solid and heavier and not enslaved but something independent of slavery, as if it were himself again, a conversion, from water to something like pudding and then butter to mud and whatever the next thing after that would be but soon after would be rock hard fall down and scrape yourself to death cement, himself and what he had inside of him all pavement, only sidewalk bounded by brief, so brief forays into the street and the sometimes soft or liquid asphalt, and when he stepped off that train, and he would hop off it as lightly as Donald O'Connor might do, that would be the end of both directions, and he would be finished.

And that indeed was how it was. He let Teddy fill him up with some very good whiskey back at the railroad house, filched a rock-hard doughnut from the plate on the table there and chewed it down, and when he got home and passed into the vestibule through the front door, he looked down at the quarts of milk souring in the crate, and bent to tap his finger on the staling crust of one of the loaves of bread. He stood, his hand on the knob of the interior door, and didn't seem to know what he must do next.

"All that for nothing," he said. And every night from now until forever, that goddamned slip.

Part Three: Paddy Dolan.

Thursday Morning: Into the Ring

That morning and a couple of houses down from Fourteen Holy Martyrs Church, Paddy Dolan woke to the smell of bacon up the back stairs as it had every morning of what had become his life in that row house on Lombard Street, a block and a half up from Union Square, an ocean away from Killarney city where he'd been born and lived to seventeen years.

As he woke, he savored the awareness of beer, girls, paycheck coming, and in celebration reached into his underwear to feel his privates. He stretched out his back and his hips, pulled at himself, then let his hand come out and his arm trail up over his torso and stretch over his head, his fingertips pressing for a moment under his nose. His own smell satisfied him, the mingling of it with the frying of bacon heartened and soothed him. Well, it was going to be another nice day. My God, how he loved this place. It was perfect.

But as the light in the bedroom grew, Paddy's mood changed to a dark and familiar thing. He had never been able to name it or know where it had come from. It was as if the light in the room was making it darker rather than brighter, that the day was going out of the room with the light. He knew if he didn't do something right now, the darkness would grow until it took him over. He shook his head, fast, took a deep breath. Familiar and regular but until today only on Sundays, not ever on a weekday. Maybe the darkness was going to try to get in every day. Now that things were his, were perfect. He panicked in the darkness, and as it always was, he believed he couldn't move, couldn't move to shake it.

The night before, that was it, something about the night. Hadn't he slept well? Had he dreamed? He didn't know. But at last he could let himself think of a shaft of afternoon light in a doorway, light on a full head of long, curly red hair, and as he did this, little by little the darkness returned to the regular light of morning.

Remembering was one of the things, like fighting, he was good at. He opened and closed his eyes now, and opened them again as if to test what he'd just done, and when satisfied all was well, swung his feet over the side of the bed, stood up, stretched, yawned, and walked past the bed and dresser into the bathroom that opened directly into his bedroom, as if nothing had passed. He didn't bother to close the door. His dad would already have gone off to his "job" sitting on a stool at his uncle's corner store, and his mother was a length of stairs away, below him in the kitchen making his breakfast. He was himself again.

"Patrick, get yourself up," he heard her call up the stairs. "I can't wait for you all the livelong morning."

"Right, then, Ma—I won't keep the sodality waiting," he yelled back down to her.

They howled. His mother hadn't been to church since they'd come to Baltimore after the war, even before Paddy had become the boxing best of the neighborhood. That was his ticket, a heavyweight champ was what he was going to be, in his mind already was. She'd go to hell sooner than let him leave the house in the morning unfed. He guessed she would even prefer it, so he was getting his breakfast and pretty well whatever else he asked for if she thought it was good for him. His dad might stay behind in the evenings when Paddy had a match on, but his mother was in the kitchen, cooking his meals and nervously standing by the wooden kitchen table while he ate. The nerves were not fussiness or sentimental. She had a sensible knowledge about whether he'd make weight for a match, and if she thought he was too far over, she'd whisk the plates away as soon as shove more of them under his nose if he was under. In the three years since he'd started boxing, during his last year at St. Martin's high school, she was only over once, and that by less than half a pound.

She should work at the ring, Paddy thought as he finished washing up. He'd like that. He'd like to always have someone by who thought as well of him as he thought of himself.

He rinsed his hands and tossed water on his face, rubbed it with the rag on the edge of the bathtub. He threw the rag on the floor as if it was his shoulder towel and he was in the ring, waiting for the bell to spring out. He boxed lightly at his image in the mirror, flicking his thumb against the side of his nose like they did in the matinee cartoons, laughed and then rumpled his own hair as if there were a father standing with him.

He dressed whistling, leaving his things on the floor and the bed unmade, jumped down the back stairs in threes and off the last step into the kitchen, smacked his mother on her backside, and sat down to a plate of eggs, bacon, and hot cakes.

"That's some swill for you," he said with a mouth full of food, and she walked over and kissed him hard on the top of his head.

Immigrants and That Bunch

Paddy had turned twenty the month before. This was his fourth spring in America. The Dolans had come over some six months or so after his dad's volunteering in the RAF, and Paddy turned seventeen the day his dad came home from the war. The first thing he said to Paddy was, "Lad, d'you remember when we'd fish up on the wall on Saturday dawn?"

He and his dad had then been about the same height and his dad had to reach up a bit to chuck him under the chin and he did that then. Paddy had said nothing, his father's touch and the intimacy of him in the room after his long absence felt disgusting, and he flinched a little, though he had tried not to. His parents both laughed in a nervous way, and then all had gone in to the prim front sitting room. He remembered how his mother had nudged Paddy, nodding toward his dad as they followed him in.

"Yeh, Da," he'd said quickly. "What was that you used to say?"

His dad cackled from between the gaps in his front teeth where the rot had gotten them in France. "Bollocks!" he laughed in triumph, wheezing over it.

Paddy threw his head back and barked out a laugh to match his dad's but the truth was that he didn't remember a lot about the years before his father left. That night he watched his mother serve the evening meal, a smile brushing the corners of her lips. Paddy found that he was sweating, that the room seemed to be darkening with a quickness that made him want to vomit. He ate nothing, and that night without understanding he pushed a straight wooden chair against his bedroom door. He woke to find the chair toppled over, all four legs just inches from the panels of the door, agape like a dog at its nap, the door slightly apart. He remembered a dream of blackness, the only image the sound of breathing, coming at him but not quite reaching him.

From that night on until they left for America he slept out, with friends or even on a spot of ground out off the main road. He'd stay with his parents during the day, but at night he was gone.

He decided to despise the free way his father had taken to tossing around vulgarities as his mother walked by them in the small, clean sitting room or the kitchen. He felt this made him a right fairy, since he knew his mother enjoyed the rough talk, but he didn't care. And he hadn't wanted to leave for America.

When his parents decided to move to Baltimore, they said they were going to go work for Paddy's brother Seamus, in a grocer's he had there. Paddy's father had had a good job driving a lorry before the war, but afterward his nerves weren't up to that or any other kind of work, it seemed. Paddy tried hard to be sympathetic, even though his dad hadn't been anything like a soldier, he bore stretchers or something like that—but he felt for sure it wasn't only due to his Dad's frailty that they were going. In fact, he knew it. One night about a month before Paddy began to stay away nights, he tried to get to sleep over the noise of his father approaching his mother in bed, a pillow over his ears and his eyes pressed into the mattress ticking, darkness ringing in them and flooding the backs of them with weird balls of light that shut out even the shadows. A minute later he heard her scream and run out of the room. She knocked into Paddy as he opened the door and she ran past him, out the kitchen and into the garden privy.

He had flushed with shame at the sight of her slim buttocks in the light that fell across the hall, and burned at the sight of his father through the doorway, grinning as he sat on the edge of their bed. He seemed to think he and Paddy were sharing some kind of joke. Then Paddy saw Nevan wore no pants, and that he held his member in one of his hands. As Paddy stood, unable to move or turn away, his father began to stroke himself, contentedly, aware of his son's eyes on him. He seemed to be inviting Paddy to something, something he should have known either to go to or run away from, but he didn't do either. He finally heard his mother's step through the back door and turned.

"You all right, Ma?" he asked quietly, glad the darkness hid his burning face. She was covered up in the old dress she kept out there on a hook.

"Sure, Pat, I just stubbed my toe in the dark." They both knew it for a lie. "If that's the worst that ever happens to me I'll be lucky enough."

His dad called out, "You comin, woman? I got to get my sleep, now, Jesus, Mary and Joseph. Send that fairy back to bed and turn out the light."

"All right, Nevan. Don't shout the house in," and she went to him and closed the door behind her.

After that night his father regularly called him a fairy, especially out in public. But Paddy wasn't a fairy, if what you meant was that he preferred boys to girls, or even if what you meant was that he was a sissy. He'd already sunk it often enough with the Bridgets and Marys and Roses at home, and now with plenty of Deborahs and Cathys and Sadies over here. A couple of times when he worried that maybe his dad was right, he even tried to think of sinking it with one of the lads, just to see if he would fancy it, but his gorge rose and the foot of his right leg flapped back and forth like a leather apron. Every time his father said it, he wanted to punch the life out him, beat him until he was pulp and put his head up on a pike as a warning to all men to never question him again. Over those months he'd had to go out and pick a fight with one of the boys, then another, then nearly every fellow in the town.

And anyway, even aside from girls, Paddy also wasn't above taking care of himself, but that didn't make a man a fairy, it just sent him to hell. In the last couple of years he really hadn't needed to, but he liked it sometimes. He enjoyed the rhythm of his own hand, his other arm thrown across his eyes, the back of his head and his heels digging into the bed. Sometimes he even gave himself a quick kiss on his the inside of his upper arm afterward as a small prize of affection.

And then occasionally, but later nearly always, when he was by himself he would think of a little girl who had lived down the road from them in Killarney, Niamh was her name, and of the afternoon one spring he had seen her in the doorway of her house, sorting flowers into a basket. She wasn't but a five-year-old, and he guessed she'd be about nine or ten now. There was something holy about her, he thought then, the light in her red curly hair, the plump little legs, the rumpled but clean pinafore over the dress. From that moment on, his favorite time of day was late afternoon, before twilight came on, and if he could remember to when the Sunday darkness came on him, he would imagine it was four o'clock in the afternoon and often this would be enough to help the dark moment pass.

He couldn't make anything of this but it didn't particularly disturb him. It was funny, though, now he came to think about it. Once a couple of weeks ago the image of her had come to him when he'd been having it on with one of the girls. He'd just had a good practice fight that afternoon, and he was celebrating. It was late at night, after ten, and somehow he wasn't getting going right away, the room they'd found was too dark, the smell of the girl pronounced, as if she was on the rag, though she'd told him she wasn't and he'd taken her word for it. She was just lying there doing nothing, her eyes planted on his face without blinking. The combination of everything must be getting to him, he thought, and so he tried to imagine the late afternoon light. The image of Niamh came to him suddenly, and immediately he felt himself harden in a way he'd never done before. The girl herself climaxed with him for the first time and so vigorously she told everyone afterward they were getting married for sure. He called her a silly bitch and laughed it off, but secretly he felt powerful, more than he ever had in the ring. Still, something he could not have named made him never want to think of Niamh again.

Still, he couldn't stop it.

After being with himself, he always lay and daydreamed of moving with his mother to one of the large green farms in

Midwest America he'd seen a picture of in the window of a travel shop. They would live there and he would fend off anybody who got too close to either of them, his dad included. They would brew their own beer in a cool cellar, and watch cyclones buzz across the skyline likes hornets looking for a sturdy place to land. It would always be dawn or late afternoon, they would always be waking up in the morning or getting ready to have tea, never working and never going to bed at night. And maybe Niamh would be with them, too, or maybe she would live nearby, the light shining always in her long red hair.

Going to bed and getting out of it was what bothered him, tell the truth.

And when that darkness came over him, he always had the one thought: that he wanted to commit murder on his father with his fists.

At home, even before this darkness had come to be regular, he already had an urge to get out, pick a fight, look for something going. But he knew what a bum he would end up if he continued that way, he'd seen enough of them in the town to know, and the one thing he had said about himself was that he was not going to end up a bum. On the other hand, the surest way to fix that and make it all respectable for yourself, if you had the fists, which he believed he most certainly did, was to sign up at the home boxing club, and he did this as soon as his dad went off to the war, though he hadn't been much more than fourteen then.

Even before he knew what he was doing, when he had what they called "no science," Paddy would pelt into the ring, fighting lads his own age and many of the older ones, beating them all bloody, each afternoon learning better the sounds and the rhythms of the ring, getting stronger and more agile, until it was as if he danced in there, humming, waiting for the hapless body parts of his opponents to saunter up to his gloves and crash into them, his chest heaving lazy and merciless. When his dad got home, Paddy knew precisely and to the second how long it would take to kill him. And one afternoon in the ring Paddy found himself imagining little Niamh sitting on a small stool at the back of the room, a light over her head, watching him and sorting flowers, and that day he nearly killed the boy he was set to fight, they'd had to pull him off the boy's neck. Some of the lads began to refuse to get into the ring with him, and the manager talked about getting him up to Dublin to work some of the circuits there.

"I tell you the truth, Nevan, that boy is something like I've never seen," the master said to his dad one night at the pub after a match. "I hate to put the other lads in with him. It's murder is what it is."

"You mean my fairy here?" his father laughed. "He's the kind of lad who pisses himself over a woman stubbin her toe." He cackled at his own cleverness, leering at Paddy. "Ain't that right, lad?"

"Ah, never mind it, Da." He tried to chuckle and struggled to keep the glass of beer he held in his hand. He tried to tell himself that it was the war, that the war had done in a lot of men. There was more, he knew it, but he couldn't get to it, he couldn't get at it in any way that would stay in his mind. He set down his glass and stood up.

"C'mon, Da, let's get you home," he said.

"No, mind you, Nevan," the master pushed on. "You'd better go on to Dublin or someplace like. That boy's not a fairy, he's a devil."

His dad roared with laughter as if this had been the best joke in world and that he himself had told it. He held on to Paddy out the door and hung on him all the way home, one hand grasping Paddy's belt buckle like a bouquet. He kissed Paddy's cheek outside the front door with a soft and wet kiss and whispered, "Goodnight, darlin." Paddy shoved him away, waited ten deadly seconds, then turned on his heel and walked away, his father's laughter following him down the walk.

The next morning when Paddy came in, his father poured him a cup of coffee without a word and then walked up to church to hear Mass. After that he didn't take a drink for a week, and by the Monday after that they were on the steamer for New York.

You Think You're Ready

After they arrived in Baltimore and his father got settled in Uncle Seamus's store, things were better. They had this spanking lovely house on Lombard Street, near Fourteen Holy Martyrs church a block up from Union Square near the hospital, and Paddy's room was down at the other end of the second floor from his parents. He had to be sure not to be in the room when his father needed to pass through to use the bathroom, but this was instinctive and not what Paddy would have put words to. There would be no more mention of fairies in public, either, though that had all but ceased once the family arrived in Baltimore.

Seamus enrolled Paddy in school, and as soon as the priest who taught physical education saw him with the gloves on, he spoke gravely to his father about his duty to further Paddy's special talent. Then Nevan, who was religious as his wife was not, began to look up to Paddy in a way that made him feel ill and keen all at once. "Fairy" became a wry joke he only used at home, said weakly with by a light cuff on the head or a feinting parry as they passed each other on the way to the kitchen. Boxing matches at school became choked with men and boys who in some cases saved streetcar money to get to the school to see him. The Gentleman's Boxing Club snatched him up as a regular the day he got his diploma, and for the past three years he had worked with Bert O'Dougal, a trainer who could have played James Cagney's grandfather. Paddy won a steady stream of small purses, but so far nothing bigger had come his way.

A week ago today, Thursday, Paddy had spoken with O'Dougal in the changing room.

"Well, lad." O'Dougal always began the transmission of information with this opening, possibly, silent as he normally was, to be certain his intended auditor realized he had begun to speak. He scratched his red, round cheek with the back of his nails, wiped his hard palm against one small, pale blue eye set almost out of the socket, belched once, patted the length of the hard full stomach that pulled out the length of his chest to his hips.

"Eh, Daddy," Paddy replied as he usually did. He wiped the sweat off his chest, thinking about the morning's match with pleasure. "That Carlson's a comer, ain't he?"

"He'll do. Don't beat him till he's useless next time, will you?" O'Dougal answered absently, taking his time. He moved his tongue inside his mouth around each one of his teeth ("Lookin for gold," he'd say sometimes), wiped both hands under its opposite armpit, hiked up the legs of his trousers to a decent height above the ankles, and sat himself down on the edge of the bench, where Paddy now bent over one knee tying a shoelace.

"You think you're ready, lad?"

Paddy straightened, puzzled. "Ready for what, Daddy?"

"For the big one." Paddy shrugged his shoulders, still perplexed. "The purse, boy. Smithie says he wants to put you up against Red Fitz Saturday week. Smithie says he wants you."

Paddy sat hard on the bench. Red Fitz was a city champion who had once put the gloves on with Rocky Marciano in a minor bout. Paddy had a signed photograph of Fitz in gloves and silks framed on his bedroom dresser. If he won—but he couldn't win. He felt a little sick.

"Nah, I can't." he said finally.

"Don't be too sure, lad. The Fitz isn't as young as he used to be, not by much he isn't." O'Dougal's eyes began to gleam. "And you've got the gloves for it, boy. I wouldn't lie to you."

Paddy took a moment. Every skinny kid in the ring could beat hell out of Red Fitz in O'Dougal's mind. But he was right that the Fitz wasn't twenty any more. Maybe Paddy could take him. And sure, even if he lost, there would be a purse of a hundred or two just from the bets on. He could take the beating, that wasn't the problem. The problem was that if he lost, that was probably it, he'd take his place in the line of trainers at the Club, and continue in neighborhood matches for a couple of years until he was too punch-drunk to go on. But if he won, that would be a whole other life—with money, to move, to get away.

"Sure, Daddy, all right. I'll do it," he said at last. *And fairy that,* he said to his father. *Fairy that, you stupid bastard.*

Thursday Afternoon: Patty's Loverboy Special

He put on his helmet and let O'Dougal lace him up, then stepped into the ring to face Smithie one more time. He thought, *Hell, yes, I'll fight you, Red Fitz. I'll fight you till the blood comes out of your teeth and the tears cascade from your eyes.* After the match, Smithie damn near dead, Paddy left the club, walked up the block, stopped at Eddie's tavern.

"Hey, lads," he called, squinting.

"Patty!" they called back. "What's new?"

He plunked down on a barstool. "Gentleman, you are looking at the next heavyweight champion of the fair city of Baltimore. Eddie, get me the usual and then some," he said.

"Hey!" they all cried, but then Old Levy, the West Side Jew, stood up. He was so short he asked for a phone book to sit on so that his elbows would reach the bar. He was the single Jew who came into in the place, famous primarily for not living on the east side and for lunching every day on ham and cheese between German rye bread. He said it was an act of revenge. He was the first customer in the morning to arrive and left promptly at 5:00 to God knew where.

"A man has got to work," he said now, as he said every day, "but you, Paddy Dolan, cannot beat Redmond Fitzhugh in the ring. His time has not passed."

"Aw, shut up, Sheenie," Greg Flathmann said. "The Club wouldn't put him up to Red if they didn't think he could do it." Greg knew this to be a lie as much as anybody, but he lived alone with his mother and it was comforting to him to say this sort of thing out loud.

"That's right," Barry Jones nodded. "They don't put 'em up until they're ready, then, if they lose, how many of 'em can beat Red after all?" Barry was a stupid son-of-a-bitch who had a knack for the obvious.

"Patty, here, that's who," Greg cried, slapping Paddy on the back. All these idiots pronounced his name that way but Levy. At this they all, but Levy, cheered and raised their glasses, and Barry called for the next round.

"Patty, boy, c'mon, show us how you took that Jackson bastard," Timmy Fitzpatrick leaned over and slurred his thick city accent down the bar.

"Yeah, Donnie, c'mon, give us the works." Richard Stone was a black-Irish looking man, not terribly tall but with the thick hair and the pale countenance over a sharp nose that proclaimed his antecedents. He always called Paddy "Donnie" though nobody knew why. He shot a straw's thickness of cigarette smoke out of his upturned face. "Show us how you flattened that nigger that one time."

Paddy smacked his glass on the bar and twirled around toward them on the stool, raising his fists. "Right, lads, one Nigger-Lover Special comin up!"

He brought down the house with that one as always, but he didn't mind coloreds and they all idolized Joe Louis. Today he didn't care about any of that shit at all. *Fairy this*, he said as he swung out at the hapless, invisible Jackson. The boys cheered, sloshed their beers on the bar, clamored for who could remember Paddy's victories the best.

Levy, it seemed, had had enough, and he stood up. "Gentlemen, it is not yet 5:00, but Paddy Dolan cannot contend with Redmond Fitzhugh. Shabbat Shalom." He ambled to the door and turned down the way.

"Somebody's going to contend with that Jew bastard one of these days if he's not careful," Eddie said from behind the bar, under the sway of irresistible emotion. Edward never commented on a customer if he could help it.

Thursday Evening: Dental Work

When he got home for dinner, he'd mostly sobered up and had forgotten all about the girl, Catherine, but he had not forgotten Petie Marlon and his insolence and was looking forward to whipping his self-satisfied ass for him. His father was already at the table, his front and chin strewn with mashed potatoes and shredded beef. "Brought some peas, lad," he said thickly, piling up a mound on his knife. He looked to be drunker than Paddy had seen him in a long time.

"Nice," Paddy replied, looking down at him. "Eh, Mam, better start window-shopping, then," he called over to his mother.

She paused at the sink, one hand on her hip, and began to give her best impersonation of Maureen O'Hara. "Now whatever would I need to waste my time for with window shopping? Am I one of these great, lazy American girls? I suppose you'd like me to take a cab home from Baltimore Street after, too? And where would I get the money for all this larking about, I'd like to know?"

She was excited, the pad of flesh around her waist vibrating a little under her house coat. Paddy thought she had probably heard about the purse before he did.

"Well, madam, yours truly will be in the fight of the century on Saturday, and there's a nice fat purse at stake with enough left over standing the lads a round for a lady to get herself a new hat. But if you'd rather not..."

"Another tooth!" Paddy's father broke in, slapping his hand mightily on the table. "Another tooth! Well, Mrs. Dolan, what do you say to that? Another of your son's teeth for the tooth fairy!"

"What are you on about, Father?" She smiled but looked puzzled, and worried.

"Every time the boy's in a fight, the bastard loses a tooth. Don't you know he still puts it under his pillow for the tooth fairy?"

"I do not!" Paddy blushed, startled at how loud he denied it. "I never—that's for babies, that is. What do you want to go on about that for, Da?"

What on earth was he on about, for Christ's sake? It was just a joke, and here Paddy was close to tears. Immediately he felt the familiar feeling, being lifted just outside the edge of the room, the darkness moving in.

"Why, sure, lad. Never you mind, but look. Here," his father answered, pulling at the small front pocket below his belt, "here's one I got off you just last week."

Paddy's mother moved in closer to take a look. "Why, it sure looks like a fresh one, darling," she said to Paddy, still puzzled.

"But I never lost a tooth, I never did."

"Sure, lad. Sure," his father said, with the ghost of a smile, "don't you remember? I thought you knew I was the tooth fairy." He looked suddenly lost, like a baby himself.

"Ah, sure, now I remember." Paddy struggled to remember even losing the tooth. There were so many holes in his mouth from lost teeth he couldn't tell. He shook his head, and grinned.

"But you never got it under my pillow. C'mon, now. O'Dougal gave it to you, right? Right?"

"Sure, lad," his father replied with a wink. "Sure. It was O'Dougal. Yeh." And he winked again, and reached over and gave Paddy's mother a little slap on her bottom. "You off, then, lad?"

"Yeh. Yeh, I'm off."

Paddy shoved a last forkful into his mouth, slurped once from the cup of boiling tea at his right hand, ran out. He was supposed to meet Edna, the cheap girl of the moment, in front of the tavern, but found himself headed south to Carroll Park, by himself, just to think, just to catch a breath. He wanted to vomit.

Thursday Night: The Purse

The air around Carroll Park on a hot summer day, when the asphalt melts into rivulets on the streets and the smell of animal dung under the trees goes from sharp to flat, was nothing like now, 11:30 on a moonlit Thursday night in April. The day had been warm, but it was cold now, and muggy. It was muggy all the time. Paddy was most aware of the single breath from the circle of boys that surrounded him. His instinct was to wait, he knew the money was his no matter what he did. One punch was all they wanted, one good slug apiece, didn't matter who got it, they were all willing to take it. The money was there in the hat. But he'd come to break Petie Marlon's ass for him, and he was going to do it.

The only thing that struck him about the boys was that Marlon was one of them, and that a tall, thin young man Paddy could never remember the name of offered him a cigarette and a light, stepping in front of Marlon as he did, and he asked him right away about the big fight, Paddy's first, on Saturday. That had broken some kind of spell, and Paddy chuckled and started right in on his sweet talk about it. Kid or no, though, kid or no, that smart-assed Marlon was going to get a piece of what he had coming to him soon, and that was a fact.

"So what'll you do then, Patty?" a fair one, Tony, asked Paddy as they circled around him in the night. He asked with a glint of something like a girl, a girl asking for how her steady had beat the shit out of some guy stupid enough to flirt with her when he knew she was taken. A cap such as an Irish cart driver might wear was glinting under the overhead light where they stood just inside the ball diamond, full of coins the boys had laid down to tell the story one more time, and he hadn't told it yet. His eye was still on Petie, who had said not a word and who had not put a penny in the cap.

"A purse, Patty," they all said again, "We got you a purse, you have to tell it, c'mon, Patty!" He would have done it for nothing, but the glint of the money made the fight with Red as real as it had been at the tavern, as real as it would be Saturday. And Marlon would be watching it all from a bed in Bon Secours Hospital if he was lucky.

Paddy raised his fists in the hundreds-year-old boxer's stance, bumping his nose with his thumb again, stamping one foot the way bulls stamp the ground with fore-hooves before the charge. Paddy even thought of it that way now: *I'm a bull, a goddamned bull.*

"So then his head'll be reeling like shit, see, and he won't be able to find his ass with both hands," Paddy started up, his eye on Marlon as if to say, "Here's what's coming, you piece of shit. Get ready to meet your maker."

It was the same story he'd told some version of or other maybe three times already, the boys were no less tired of hearing it now than then. He'd tell it a half-dozen times more before Saturday night when he faced Red in the ring downtown. He'd tell it after morning Mass to Monsignor Hayes and the cluster of altar boys and grade school kids who would have come to Saturday Mass because they knew he'd be there. He wouldn't have a beer tomorrow, but he'd stop by Eddie's again and as many other corner taverns as he could fit in. He'd go over it another three times easy with O'Dougal, if his heart hadn't already given out from pride.

"And then I'll give him my right, right above the belt, and that'll be it. Himself down like a truck full of horse shit!" he shouted the same way he had crowed it to his mother. He thought about her now with pride and pleasure, and then of Niamh. He took a breath, got ready for the big finish.

"And then what'll you do, pussy? Beat up a little girl?" Marlon slurred this at him in his slow way, light from the streetlamp in his thick blonde hair, cigarette smoke spewing in two fast straight streams from his nostrils.

And the scene froze, the boys and Paddy's good right suspended before his face. A few of them had been with Paddy down at Catherine's yard this afternoon, but nobody thought Marlon was asshole enough to do anything else about it. They were surprised Paddy hadn't killed him right then and there, and admired his restraint when Petie strolled up, before Paul had stepped forward with the cigarette. "Saving it up for Red," they thought to themselves. Sure, who would waste it on a lunatic like Marlon? That boy was out of his mind when it came to Catherine, flat-chested goody-two-shoes none of them would waste a breath on. Anyway, Paddy had just been teasing her some, she was so stuck-up, she could dish it out but she couldn't take it. They waited.

Paddy dropped his hands. "You want to say that again?" He smiled at Petie.

"You heard me." And Petie was not smiling at all, looking older than himself to Paddy, something even attractive about him, and Paddy flushed with shame and rage.

"Say it again, boy. I dare you."

The other boys had stepped out of the circle, not one wanting this now, not for Petie, nor for Paddy, and the hope of the one good punch they did want evaporated like steam out of a manhole cover in winter.

"What are you, deaf?" Petie threw down his cigarette and stubbed it out like a New York City cop at the pictures, said into the ground, "Huh—the man's not only a pussy, he's a deaf pussy."

It took the one hard right to knock him down, and the way his head flew back the boys were surprised Paddy hadn't knocked it off or at the very least broken his neck, but Petie was still conscious enough to roll into a ball where he fell. It wasn't any good. It took three minutes, maybe five, for the rest of the boys to get Paddy off him. Paddy had broken his hand on Petie's jaw and it was blooming like a purple cabbage, but that didn't stop him. He kicked Petie, beat him with the broken hand and the good one, tried tearing his shoulder off with his teeth, got a good bite out of it, even. He kneed him in the stomach, in the groin, battered his chest with his head. He was sobbing, "Call me a fairy, goddamn you, call me a fairy, fairy this you bastard, you cunt..." and kept sobbing as the boys managed to throw him off to the side at last.

He got to his feet, raised his bloody fist in the air just as Petie has raised a brick that afternoon in Catherine's yard, cried out, "Who's next? Who wants it next?" and most of the boys scattered. He stood then, alone save the broken boy moaning in the grass and two who stayed to crouch by to make sure Paddy didn't hurt him anymore. The air should have been punctuated with the song of crickets, but there was none, only the street lamp buzzing a little in the humidity. Finally one of boys stood, picked up the hat, said, "Take it."

And, not knowing why, Paddy took it.

He wandered through the night-blackened streets, pausing now and again under a street lamp, the capful of coins hanging in his left hand. Wilkins Avenue, always bright with traffic and noise and people coming and going, was nearly dead with quiet, and seemed like a foreign country. He turned up Fulton Avenue, his right hand paining him nearly to the point of passing out, the weight of the coins in his left becoming such a burden over those few blocks that he wanted to set them down on the pavement, but he could not bring himself to do it. The purse was propelling him home.

His mouth was dry, he could hear his breath. The night was a creature that had left him alone on the street, and the darkness was not a part of him but its own being. A few bugs flickered around the street lamps, and the cement of the pavements grew sharper as he walked in and out of the lamplight, brighter, then grey, then nearly black. A dog barked.

He was just a lad, that Petie Marlon. Paddy didn't even really know him. He hadn't ever before walked up that alleyway on Stricker, and as he thought this, he turned away and back again down to Pratt Street, past his uncle's store, down to the corner of Stricker. He looked up the street. He didn't know which house was hers, or which was Petie's. He could walk up Stricker and pass both their houses, yet he couldn't do that. He turned on his heel again, up Pratt, to Fulton, to Lombard and home. He wanted to make the sign of the cross as he passed in front of Fourteen Holy Martyrs, but that would have meant dropping the cap or crossing himself with his left hand, and he couldn't do either. He thought the pain in his hand might really be killing him.

He let himself in the front door, walked back to the kitchen, dropped the hat of coins on the table, and turned on the faucet to clean the right hand where it had broken open. He couldn't feel it anymore, but it was twice the size and he could see from the way the joints twisted he'd never use it in the ring again. He found a towel, wrapped it around the hand tight enough that he nearly vomited into the sink and had to catch himself so he wouldn't fall down. The room went black at the edges, then at the center, and then he was all right. He picked up the hat with his left and it still felt heavy out of all proportion.

He climbed the back stairs, hat in his hand, defeat pressing on him with the weight of the coins. He wanted to drop it, it felt so heavy again, but he couldn't, the purse was steering him to some place he had to be. He turned left on the little landing and stepped up to his room. The light from the alley lamp threw a beam over the coverlet of his bed, where his father was stretched out, one arm over his eyes. Paddy stood, white in sweat, a buzz in his ears. The entire world turned dark and small and far away.

"D'you win, lad?" his father asked without moving.

"Aye, Da. I won." He spoke with the Irish lilt he'd left behind three years ago, as if he were a little boy and his father asked him if he'd made it up to confession.

"Nice purse, then?"

"Pretty good, I think. Haven't counted it yet."

"Ah."

Paddy waited. He knew, though beyond memory, real consciousness. But as a photo album he had not been able to open before and had put up in a tin cupboard, he had stumbled upon it after forgetting it was there, and it had come untied before him, without his doing, the black ribbons of closure hanging like spittle, his early life mocking him as it undid him. Now he remembered, these not like other memories but bits of photographs, cut and blown up and scattered across the world: his dad in his room at night, using him, cackling and grunting over him, front or back, but as if he, Paddy, were not there, as if he could have been anybody, man, woman, beast. He remembered the next mornings, his father pouring him out a little coffee or tea in an attitude of courtesy, like a courtesan who had to be paid and treated well in the morning even if you had beat her in the night. He remembered running down the alley to get to school and falling, scraping his knee bloody and sharp, and crying as if someone had died.

He remembered vomiting the day of his first penance, the hand of the priest hard on his neck as he spilled out his guts over the vestry floor. He remembered trying to tell his mother, and her interrupting him with the news that his father was going off to war, and that they might never see him again. He remembered all the beautiful days and nights of being able to sleep on his back with the door unlocked and unbarred while his father was gone, and every single sinew in his father's throat, every black pore on his nose and chin. The room darkened again.

He walked around the bed to the window, sat down on the edge of the bed, his torso turned a little to face his father, the hat purse still hanging from his left fist.

"Hey, lad."

Paddy didn't answer.

"Hey, lad. Can't you help out your old man, boy."

Paddy shifted a little on his right hip, tossing the hat up over his right arm and on to the dresser at the foot of the bed. He turned back around, and with his left hand felt for the buckle of his father's pants. He undid the buckle, and slid the belt out of the loops with a couple of tugs. His father lifted his hips to help, but didn't move his arm from over his eyes. Paddy tossed the belt on the floor like the brassiere of a lover, then climbed into the bed next to his father. He laid his head on his father's breast, tucking his right arm underneath him, letting the weight of the pose pound blood and agony into the broken hand. He unzipped his father's trousers with his left hand, his left arm reaching the length of his father's torso to find inside his trousers. He lifted out his father's penis, and with the rhythm of long practice, began to stroke. A single sob broke from him. His father lifted his arm from his eyes, still closed, and gently stroked Paddy's hair where it lay below his chin.

Friday Morning: Pause for Seamus

Seamus stood behind the counter, swaying, pushing his left foot into the floor board that weaved and creaked under his weight, enjoying in his mind the two young men who had just left the store, enjoying their insults and their laughter. He spent ten minutes suppressing any thought more particular about Paul, who he felt was just the perfect age for a young man to be, than that he'd like to take him out bowling, or maybe to the fights, or even to the pictures. He didn't let himself think more than that, and had no idea that the thoughts and feelings hidden from himself were available to read over his face like a map to anyone who had seen them before and knew what they meant. Seamus was a grown man, a good fifteen years older than his brother Nevan. He was married, he'd lost a son in the same war his brother had fought in, and had a daughter who lived out in Hagerstown, and he ran this corner store. He wasn't a queer, though. He was not a queer.

If he'd let himself think about the matter at all, he would have said it was his brother who was a little funny, but he would not have been able to tell you why he had said so.

A shadow covered the light coming in the door for just a moment, and Paddy came in. Seamus smiled, pleased to see him.

"How are you this morning, lad?" he asked, flushing like a shy girl as he always did when he addressed his nephew.

"I need—" Paddy began, then stopped. "My da," he tried again, and stopped.

"What is it, Paddy? What's wrong with your da?" Seamus moved quickly and was out from behind the counter in a few steps.

"He, uh, he's buggared—I mean, he's in the tub, my mam is up there with him, you'd better go."

"Jesus," Sean said. He'd just gotten sight of Paddy's useless fractured hand. "He do that to you, lad?"

"What? Yeah, yeah, he did, I was trying to fight him off — no, I don't remember. It wasn't him. I don't know what happened."

"What do you mean, lad? Did he put hands on you? Did he hit you? What did you do?"

And this was how it always was, Paddy never being able to say what anybody had really done. No one had done anything by the time it was all over anyway. Nobody ever said a word.

Least said, soonest mended, he thought. *You remember that, Niamh. It's the best way.*

He pulled himself together, looked at his uncle, saw him blush, turned up one corner of his mouth. "Get me a cigarette, sir, would you?" he asked, making the "sir" nearly another insult. "My father is dead in the bathtub. I don't know how it happened. Maybe he seized up, or had a heart attack. I can't tell to look at him. Will you come up and help my mother, sir?" This time the word was not an insult. "She's up there with him alone, she told me to come fetch you."

"Yes, of course. Let me just tell Maura I'm going," he said, and disappeared into the store again.

"Whatever! Whatever is the matter!" Paddy could hear his aunt crying from inside, and then his uncle's lower and muf-fled reply, and then in the wailing that followed, his uncle came though the passageway again.

"Let me just lock this up, now. We'll go out the front and around," he said.

Paddy's arm was killing him and his arms and face were still covered in dirt and blood, though he had put on clean clothes. They walked the block up Gilmore. Paddy didn't think a hill had ever felt so difficult to walk but when they turned on to Lombard, the sweet flatness of that street felt even heavier to him, and looked darker. The sun was just beginning to come up over the houses and a few shafts of light might hit the top of one's head or the bricks to one's left, but this didn't give him the pleasure it should. *Waking up. Now that's gone, too.*

They let themselves into Paddy's house, turned the skeleton key in the vestibule door, walked into the parlor. It seemed to be ready for a death, Seamus thought, spotless and demonstrating no individual taste of photographs or plants or flowers, not even anything particularly telling about the furniture than that its owners were frugal to the point of meanness: one small settee against the wall facing the mantelpiece, the ubiquitous glass ashtray in a silver stand, and three hardwood chairs arranged variously in front of the windows. Even the stairway was not as fine as many you would see in a Lombard Street house: a plain recessed bit of a hallway with the stairs going straight up until they turned sharply, no banister, no newel post. A radio, the sole concession to ease, because Finola liked to listen to the fights and baseball games on it, stood on a metal table as many people kept in their kitchens. Next to the radio was a statue of the Blessed Virgin as she appeared on the Miraculous Medal, with her palms outstretched and the elegant foot of one leg pressing into the head of a serpent. The wallpaper had originally been some kind of floral from two decades ago, now was nearly brown with water stains and age.

Seamus followed Paddy up the stairs, turned left on the landing toward the large bedroom. Paddy said nothing, so he called out, "Finola? Are you all right?"

She came running through, her arms stretched out straight, "Oh, Seamus, it's our poor Nevan dead. He's dead, I think he's dead, Seamus, come quick."

She pushed Paddy aside to make way for his uncle, so that Paddy was following last behind them into the back bedroom, where he saw his uncle stiffen just for a moment as he entered that room, not enough that most would have noticed it, but enough for Paddy to see. In fact, the smell of spent ejaculation hit Seamus like drink, that smell that made his wife sick if it lingered in underclothes or on sheets for too long.

He turned to Paddy. "You sit down here on the bed and wait," he ordered, and not at all to his surprise, Paddy, who had grown more diminished with each step up the stairs, did as he was told. He couldn't know that the thought of his nephew sitting on that bed excited his uncle, and that his confidence, taking over for them, had only to do with this excitement.

Finola paused before the door, turned, looking small and frail, and said to Seamus, "I don't think I can go back in there."

"No, it's no place for you. I'll go," he said. "You wait here with the boy."

She turned, sat down next to Paddy, did not touch him.

Seamus felt a relief such as he'd never felt. His erection was growing into something painful and he had not known how he was going to keep it from his sister-in-law, but now that was all right. He could even leave the door open behind him, as if he had nothing to hide, which pleased him so much he could barely move. The erection dissipated at the sight of his brother's body in the tub, yet he reached out for the basin and cried out as if he were spent, and he heard Finola in Paddy's bedroom begin to weep at the sound of his cry.

The last time Seamus had felt anything so repulsive he had been in bed with a woman with whom he'd finally been able to be satisfied only after seeing her little boy peek his head in on them and had scurried right away when Seamus looked up at him. He had married Maura instead of that woman, and she had made no demands on him whatever, and had been completely pleased when he stopped coming to her after their daughter was born. From that time to this he had not felt such a sensation, and this one filled him so completely he wondered how he would live to speak of it to anyone, or to whom indeed he could speak it.

The sightlessness that followed the experience passed, and he felt himself grow cold, and filled with greater shame.

Then he heard Finola calling to him, "Seamus? Can you tell what did it?"

"I'm sorry, lass. I was just looking at him then. I'll see."

He heard her begin to cry again, as if the suggestion of his own incapacitation and grief let her show hers the more.

He turned on the tap, rinsed his hands, put his fingertips to Nevan's throat to feel a pulse, though he knew there would not be one: the discharge from the man's bowels, which oddly he could see but not smell, told him he was dead. As a very young man he had been a medic in the Great War, and he knew the signs. The color of Nevan's skin and the expression on his face said he had died of a heart attack, apparently after drawing himself a bath. It wasn't uncommon: it happened all the time. One moment you were leaning over to turn off a faucet, the next you were gone. He was gone.

Seamus checked himself again. He could feel a bit of light sticky film on his leg, but his clothes appeared dry and clean. He would have to remember to hide his undershorts away from Maura. He knew he would need to keep them.

He went out to the woman and her son. Like a physician, he told them, "It was his heart. There was nothing anyone could have done. We had better call the undertaker and get things ready."

Finola turned to Paddy. "His heart," she said, "Something broke his heart." She got up, said, "I need my coin purse," and went out of the room.

"I'll go over to the funeral home in a little bit," Seamus told Paddy. "Don't worry about a thing. And we'll get the fight postponed, that will be all right."

Paddy looked up to him. "Fight? I'm not ever going to fight again."

Friday Afternoon: Let Them Dream

After the girl left him, Paddy moved his hand from his thigh down to the slats of the park bench. He had to force himself not to slam it into the dark green paint. He couldn't think, there was nothing left to think. Flowers were beginning to push up between the cracks in the path, little violets and what looked like could be buttercups. He dug the toe of his lace-up boot into some just in front of him and the delicate yellow and purple petals crushed themselves into faint stains in the concrete.

He was hungry. His mother had not made him breakfast.

How dared she?

He wasn't himself. The girl had been pleasant. No budding of her figure yet, he noticed, though she was tall. She wasn't very pretty, he thought, but she was sweet. Concerned, and vulnerable, eager to please, and he liked that. Then he thought, *I could make use of that*. That was a novel idea. He noticed she'd walked down Stricker. He could walk that way now, pass by her window, she might notice him. No, that wouldn't be too smart, would it? Familiarity provided opportunity for reflection, except, of course, when it didn't.

Let her dream. This was also a novel thought. It pleased him, he worked it around in his mind for a while. *Yes, she can dream still.*

By God, he was hungry. He stood, looked through the handful of scattered trees over to the houses on Hollins. That newspaperman still lived over there, but he was old, he was past it. Gave some respectability to the place, though. He scanned the row of pristine houses, the immaculate white and red steps that led up to each, the elegant molding that settled above each topmost floor. The sun dappling through the thin limbs of the park trees on to the brick fronts in the slant of the early afternoon. Something good was about to happen, of that he felt certain. He looked the other way, over to Carmen's house in the middle of the far block.

He'd had her a couple of times, behind a tavern usually, but he knew where she lived. She'd never brought him up, though, said she had kids. He didn't care about kids, he told himself.

He shook his head. What had he been thinking of? Oh, yes. His Niamh. It was foolish of Paddy not to have seen before. He bet it was because she'd cut her hair recently, or maybe even that the sunlight in this neighborhood didn't show the bobbed ends off to advantage, almost yellow when the full sun hit their brown depths and waves, but now that he'd seen her truly, he was happy again. And he'd never hurt her again, he was positive of that.

Those thick black eyebrows of hers, though. He'd like to put them between his lips, pull at them, or — well, no, he couldn't do that. Not to his Niamh. She was Niamh and he was Oisin, and he had travelled across the Eastern Sea to this rot of a place, and he was going to have it his way or none.

"Jesus Christ, you're an Irish fecking idiot," he said to himself in somebody else's voice. But he loved this place, after all, he was at home here. And he was king here, wasn't he? Over there was a dream, this was real. Even the beer, he'd had to grow used to it at first, but now he loved it, the bitterness of it and manufactured sameness of the taste. And he was going to do murder on Red Fitz with his hands. He looked down at his hands. He couldn't feel them, and wondered if a beer would bring the feeling back.

"Fuck them," he said aloud. "Fuck them north, south, east, and west. Fuck them 'till they're dead," he said to himself.

Friday Night: I Had To, Man, He Went for Me

The sun was going down, the bench was cold, several people had passed Paddy, looked over at him, and he thought someone might have even said something to him, but he couldn't move, not a bit. He would just stay right here, he thought. All the afternoon, it wouldn't leave him be, he couldn't put it away from him.

But his Da. That's right. That's why he was sitting here, why he'd been here since the morning, hungry, his broken hand in his lap. And he remembered it all. He couldn't forget any of it now, though his memory had been gone, or hidden, or something, for the last ten years anyway.

"Jesus fucking Christ," he said out loud, and looked at his hands again.

Not too many hours since he'd been tempted to cut them off at the wrists, they hurt so. He'd awakened in the morning with his face buried in the rag he'd wrapped his broken hand with, the hand pressed between his nose and the pillow. He could feel the waist of his shorts tight under his buttocks. His left arm was twisted under his torso and dead asleep. As he came to, he pumped his hips into the mattress a couple of times, and then the pain of his hand and the numbness of the other arm coming to life hit him simultaneously. He couldn't have said which of the two was worse, but whatever else he might have thought or felt, all was lost in that pain.

He breathed in, his mouth still on his hand, and that slight movement nearly sent him back to unconsciousness. He tried to lift his head, felt the still useless and numb left arm begin to return to circulation, first the tingling, then the buzz, then the searing long pain he thought might actually kill him. He realized he had to turn over on to his back at least, or he didn't know what would happen to him. He pushed down on the right forearm to free the left, cried out, and sank once back into the pillow, where he could now smell sour spit and blood and something else—shite? How in God's name had he gotten shite on his hand? He wanted to retch. He tried pushing up again, screamed low with his mouth closed, finally flipped over on to his back.

He was naked but for the shorts twisted and stretched below his privates. The pain coming from it seemed everywhere was nothing like anything he'd felt in the ring or out, and that was saying something. It was too dark to see the broken hand, but he knew it must still be twice the size or better. He'd broken bones in that hand before. Maybe it was how he'd slept on top of it. Maybe more than one bone was broken—maybe all of the bones were broken. *Shit.* Maybe he should take himself to Bon Secours, but how would he get there? Did he have carfare? He couldn't think. The hand was hot. The left arm was only tingling now, had lost the feeling it had become boneless or that bone was regenerating in useless flesh. He could use that elbow to raise his torso, the hand to get his legs over the side of the bed.

He sat, the back of the right forearm laid down across his thighs. He stared into the blood and rag-strafed palm that looked like it had been pumped full of air, or jelly. He found if he breathed slowly then rapidly, back and forth like that, it took some of the edge off the pain. His head was fit to burst, he said to himself.

And then he thought of how he had fallen asleep in his father's arms a few hours before, how he'd found himself when he wakened. He remembered the agony of pulling himself carefully out from under his father's shoulder so as not to wake him from the erotic coma into which he had fallen, of sitting on the edge of the bed, looking out of the space between the window shade and the sill.

Everything had seemed then to be sharper and larger than it really was, and it seemed that way now, too, as he sat in the same place and in the exact same attitude, the only difference being that before the room had been dark but for the starlight and lamplight that came in, and now the sun was coming up in earnest. He saw the paint mildly cracking on the window sill, the slight smudges on the pane of the window, a tiny cobweb clinging to the screen behind the glass. When he looked beyond it he saw the bricks of the back of the house next door deep in shade, and further out, the sunlight hitting a far stretch of houses.

And he stood, peered through the window, and then Paddy felt his father's arm creeping around his waist again, and he turned violently around, but his father was not there. All at once he took the three steps into the bathroom running, and threw himself over the toilet, retching up the bile that was all that was left in his stomach. As he heaved, he became aware that water was running in a stream from the tub faucet, and as he looked up, saw his father asleep there, naked from the waist down, half-deep in water. How could that be? Paddy reached over and turned the faucet off. The water was icy, but his dad hadn't wakened in it. Paddy stood, pulled his shorts up to his waist, flushed the toilet, turned on the light, bent to his father.

"Da?" he whispered. The flesh on his father's face was blue. "Da."

Paddy sat on the edge of the tub. The water was draining and he couldn't see but could smell that his dad's bowels had emptied under him. "So pissed he's shit himself." That's what he let himself think, but he knew already that wasn't what had happened.

He stood, nearly blacked out, bent to retch again, didn't bother to flush after himself this time. He turned, left the room and his dad lying there, passed through the upper floor to the door of his parents' bedroom, tried the handle, found the door locked. He rapped with his left.

"Mam?" He called out the word softly, the way he muttered it to himself in the ring, so that the fellows all thought he was saying, "Man," like a beatnik or maybe it was some goddamned Irish thing, they thought, like calling every mother's son "lad" no matter how old he was. Or saying who he was, that he was a man, because he was a kid finding a way to turn himself into a man, and they all understood, and pitied, and tolerated, and determined to beat it out of him if they got the chance.

Where was she?

"Mam!" he cried out. Why wouldn't she come to the door?

The light changed then, slow but astonishing, light filled the landing, and he couldn't believe it but now he could see the halo around Niamh's head. He could see Niamh. It was she, she was looking over at him. *We played in the dark on Jermyn Street, knowing we had something that would last a long time. Watching Niamh laugh at you from the doorstep her mother wouldn't let her go farther than, where she was safe, you knew she was safe and that made you safe, too, and how pretty she was, how beautiful, her hair like that, curled, red, soft, the little stray wires shining in relief around the round silhouette so that you could almost count them, almost reach out and feel them, sometimes brass, sometimes looking soft as a red felt hat or the stray strands of carded wool that had yet to make their way onto a knitting needle. You'd laugh up at her, and push off the fellow who'd knocked you down in the game, and it would be perfect, and natural, as if God had made one race of people, one age, and they all saw the world the same, and asked the same things of it, and of each other. And now she was calling you, "Paddy," though you'd never heard her use your name before and hadn't known she knew it and somehow that thought turned your stomach and you wanted to retch, it was*

"Mam," he muttered from the floor where she bent over him, shaking his shoulder, calling his name. "Mam."

"What is it, Patrick? What's the matter, darling?"

She reached for his hand to squeeze, he screamed then at the touch of it and felt her pitch back as if he'd struck her. Where was Niamh? How would he keep her safe? She was asking him something but he couldn't make it out—but then it seemed it wasn't his Niamh after all, it was his mother, and she'd come to the door, and she would take care of it all now, and he could tell her. But he had to be sure Niamh was safe. He'd tell, that's what he'd do, he'd tell Mam and she'd make sure everyone was safe, yes. He opened his eyes, looked at her through trusting tears, as if he were five again and had fallen and scraped his leg open, and he saw her eyes soften to him, and knew that he could say what had happened.

"Mam, he went for me. He went for me, Mam, he went for me."

"Who went for you, lad? What are you talking about? What's wrong with your hand, my God, Patrick?"

He couldn't see her properly. The light around Niamh was making everything else so dark. He couldn't make the words come out the way he wanted them to.

"He went for me, I couldn't hit him, I couldn't, Mam, I wanted to but I couldn't."

"No, no, you couldn't, lad, of course you couldn't."

He couldn't believe it. She knew then, she understood, she knew what he was talking about, she'd help him, and then they'd go away and take Niamh with them and they could just leave that sod there in the tub to rot until he was safe in hell. He felt joy then, because she knew, because he had finally said it right and she had understood. And now he could say it as much and as loud and as often as he wanted. He smiled up at her, brilliant, and he saw her shudder even as she smiled back at him.

"Let's get him, Mam, he's in the tub, let's go get him."

"In the tub! What are you talking about, Patrick Nevan! There's nobody in the tub this time of the morning. Try to make some sense, boy, tell me what's happened."

"Sure, Mam, it's Da, he went for me, he's in the tub."

"Your *Da!*" she cried to him then. "What do you mean, your Da went for you?"

Ah, no, no, no, no, no, sure, she must have known that's what he meant, she must have known! *Come on, Mam,* he wanted to say, *come on, you knew, then, didn't you know? You knew. Mam.*

But when she sat back on her heels then, still staring at him as if she couldn't understand him, he saw what she'd always kept on her face, what let her to lock her bedroom door against the sounds of her husband taking her son in her place. And that was as far as he could go, the last lucid thought he could muster.

He thought of Petie Marlon, sobbing on the baseball diamond down in Carroll Park, and then thought, *What am I saying?*
Of course I went for him, of course I hit him. I murdered the bastard. And
I'll murder that bastard Red Fitz as well, and we'll take the purse, the
three of us, and we'll get out of here. He turned to Niamh, smiled at
her, sweetly, and at his mother, but with the same ugly smile he
wore last night, and he saw her feel what that smile meant as she
rose to her feet. He felt brilliant. They were bloody brilliant, all
of them, he knew it.

"Tell me who you're talking about, Patrick."

He couldn't stop smiling, not then. "It's Petie, Mam. He's in
the tub. I think he's dead."

Saturday: The Wake

After having vowed that he would kill the motherfucker who
had trod on his hand if he ever saw him again, Paddy had at last
gotten up from the bench and gone home and sat all night in the
living room, where his father's body would have been had they
still been back at home, and where his mother had placed a sick-
ening array of hot-house flowers and plants on the wooden table,
moved to the center of the room. She sat in one chair, straight-
backed, and he sat in another. His uncle Seamus sprawled on
the sofa, every now and again sighing deeply, whistling through
his teeth, and adjusting his trousers at the crotch. Fiona kept
a coffee pot going, filling up white glass coffee cups for Paddy
and Seamus. Paddy's hand, he could feel, was slowly turning to
cement, and in his head he played the radio as it would sound
broadcast from the boxing match on that night, inserting some
other name where "Dolan" ought to have been, and by the early
hours his rage had grown into a thing that even he could not
compass.

This morning he entered Eddie's tavern to find Levy sitting on his phone book on his stool, and although Levy didn't look up, Paddy said in his general direction, "If you say one word to me, Jew, I will fucking make you wish you had never seen the prick-clipped light of day."

Levy didn't so much as move his head, but Eddie moved over to where Paddy started to take a stool and said low, "Here, you can't talk like that in here, Patty. This is a decent place. I don't hold with them myself, but he's a regular customer and nobody has to go for that kind of talk."

"Feck yourself," Paddy said, turned on his heel, and walked out.

"Tscheeze," Eddy said, wiping down the bar. Levy tapped the end of his beer glass on the counter, ready for the next.

Saturday Night: Love's Young Dream

Go, go, go, go, go, go, go, *go*.

There, finally, Jesus.

Paddy pulled himself off Carmen and his elbows felt like the skin had been rubbed right off them. Well, that had been absolutely nothing to write home about, though he had screwed her as hard as he could manage and she had laughed the whole time. Too bad, he had thought for sure it would be about the best he'd had. He scratched at the flesh of his hand underneath the bandage she had put on it, after she'd made him take a bath, but since that had meant her soaping him all over and talking dirty in his ear while she did it, letting him play with her titties and ending with her hand on his thing, that had also been all right, way better than all right. Maybe that was why. Maybe she had taken all the life out of him.

That hadn't been what it was, though, he knew from long experience that wasn't what it had been. When they entered the apartment, he couldn't believe it, but there was Niamh again, sitting on the sofa, playing with some paper dolls or something. How in the name of God Carmen had gotten hold of her, he couldn't tell you, but he was overjoyed, though she had not so much as raised her head to look at him or say hello. This must be their secret, he thought. He would not show how he felt. And, in the back of his mind, sure it was he didn't want Niamh to know the kind of thing he was doing with Carmen, he didn't want to make her jealous, or, heaven forbid, anger her.

"Say, lover boy," Carmen said not in his direction but looking up at the ceiling, as if someone's head were up there, "that was a good one, wasn't it?"

Paddy didn't know if she was making fun, or what.

Part Four: Petie.

Thursday Afternoon: Sister

Petie bounced away down the alley, a little on his toes and letting his hips swing just a bit—not in a girlish way, but powerful, everything just up in front. Whatever was coming after today, it was going to be good. He'd have to take a hit from Paddy Dolan now, and he wasn't happy about it—but, he said to himself, let's face it, everybody has to take a hit once in a while. His older brother was going over there to Korea, and he wasn't going to no picnic, and he might be there a while. And this kind of thing, that's what made you tough. He was ready.

He thought about Catherine next door. *My God, she's skinny*, he thought, but what he meant was, *My God, she's just a kid*. Until this afternoon he'd always thought of her as being smarter than him, much wiser, and older than him, too. That's why he was always showing off to her, keeping her guessing, never letting her know when he'd be around. It was the only leverage he had. When he had upped the story to hanging alley cats in the doorways of people he didn't even know, it was because it would shock her, and he wanted to shock her. Every day he figured would be the last he'd see her. She'd go on to high school, get a job on Baltimore Street or downtown, maybe she'd even move out somewheres far like Reisterstown or Catonsville or some damn place. And then what? He'd be done for, that's what. He didn't know what that meant, he just knew it was true.

And then this here had happened and he didn't know what to think exactly any more. Until Paddy had come into her back yard just now and swore at her, he'd never thought about her as someone anybody else even knew, really. She was a little sister, someone to tease, push around, because that was who he was and what he got to do. He had never thought about her one way or the other from the shoulders down, but now he came to think of it some more, she really was kind of a skinny little thing. He'd noticed when she was playing with the jump rope that she was pretty well all arms and legs, but he never thought of her as a girl, only as herself, as his, like his German shepherd or his parents. He didn't much care for skinny girls, really, now he came to think about it, but it seemed to suit her, he thought. He had been shocked that Paddy had even referred to her chest, much less had made fun of it, but when he did, that was it and that's when he knew: he owned Catherine, she belonged to him, she was beautiful, and if he had to, God knew he'd defend her against a bastard like Paddy Dolan.

But while he was standing there with the screen door between him and Catherine after Paddy had taken off, something changed, or added to it all, or something else, he wasn't really sure. He saw that the second button to her blouse had come undone, and he saw her slip underneath it. It was cotton, white, a tiny bit of lace on it, the top not sewn in a heart shape or divided-like, the way the ones in the Sears catalogue often were, but just straight across, like an old lady undershirt. It wasn't seeing the slip that had shocked him, though, nor that there was nothing rising up out of it. It was that Catherine didn't have anything else on under the slip. Though she was flat as a pancake and would not have been the kind of girl who would have been wearing a brassiere in the first place, the thought of her skin just underneath that slip all on its own just about did him in, and it all had taken less than a second. He was sweating from the mess with Paddy and his crew already, but he tasted the salt sweat on his mouth when he licked his lips, he felt like she had put the sweat there, that it might even be hers.

And then that thing happened to him. He had to get his hand inside that slip, and he almost felt like he would hurt her to do it. The voice he'd used when he had spoken to her, the words he'd said: it wasn't him. It didn't feel like him, and yet it did. He had kept his voice low and his eyes on that crest of white cotton under her blouse, and all the time the thought of her naked skin underneath the slip had made him feel like a fire engine, a train on rails, electricity cascading off the intersection of a trolley car and its connecting wire. The thing was so beyond his ability to say he didn't know how he'd even been able to form the sounds to demand of Catherine that she let him in.

Then he'd heard her mother's key in the front door and immediately snapped out of it. He thought he must have gone nuts for a minute, mentally retarded or something. There she was, Catherine, just in front of him, and she was a skinny kid again, and all he wanted to do was get off those steps. For a stupid minute he thought, *It's these goddamned steps theirselves are the trouble.* He'd threatened Paddy like an asshole standing on them, and now he was looking at getting the shit kicked out himself for it. And he'd had to push Catherine up them to get her out of the way in the first place. That must mean something. He didn't know for sure, but he bet that was it. All he knew was, once he got himself off those goddamned steps, he was himself again.

Thursday Evening: They Just Tell You What

All these things kept going through his mind as the shade formed by the movement of the late afternoon sun played its way over the houses and streets as it always did, front to back. The air smelled damp, but good, a little bit fresh but with just enough scent of gasoline and tar in it to make it comfortable. He saw an old man walk a cart of newspapers and rags down the street and thought, *I'm ona go down the B&O a while.*

He crossed over Pratt and headed down Calhoun. It took him about seven minutes to reach the railroad yard. His friend Teddy would not be there, so he'd have to make do with jumping a car if there was one. When he was on shift, Teddy was in charge of closing the car doors shut, pulling over the long iron rod through the hole in the latch with a long smooth motion that Petie admired. Teddy would let Petie jump on the caboose car on a train headed north, and it didn't take long before the train was riding through Lake Roland, and Teddy would slow it down again and Petie would jump off and roll down into the ditch off the side of the tracks. He'd just go up there to think sometimes. He wouldn't run into anybody, usually, but he'd find things and see what he could make of them. Lots of cigarette butts and beer bottles and flat whiskey bottles with not a drop of drink left in them. Shoes, almost always sneakers, never a whole pair, and he'd always wonder how a person wound up losing one shoe and moving on without it and what the heck they were doing when they lost it. Sometimes he saw animal scat, mostly dogs but sometimes from some other animal that he wouldn't know what it was but he'd pretend mountain lion or bear or something equally improbable. And then the one time that pair of girl's glasses in nearly perfect shape that sat on top of his chest of drawers in his bedroom at home, the arms folded under in perfect symmetry and looking like a patent leather moth waiting to take off.

He never hung back from the train cars, he wouldn't have cared if somebody saw him and he wouldn't have dashed away running, either. Most of the gentlemen that worked the lines knew him and liked him, and unless there was a boss around they had to watch out for they never yelled at him to get lost.

Tonight as he walked into the yard he saw Larry, an older man with one good leg and one wooden. Larry always smelled a little bad, and he had said to Petie on a more stultifying and hot day than usual last July, when Petie had come up to him and then taken a hasty step back away, that where they had taken his leg off in France it had never healed up right and was always seeping out a little bit. "I treat it with some powder but I run out last week," he said, and Petie had reached quickly into his trousers and found fifteen cents.

"Go head," Petie had told him. "If anybody comes I'll say I ain't seen you. Damn, that is bad, boy," and he held his fist up to his mouth and pressed his lips into his teeth. Larry had shuffled away fast in the direction of Baltimore Street, and when he got back about forty-five minutes later, he looked happy and smelled brighter, and invited Petie into the night's pinochle game. He lost one hand to him for precisely fifteen cents, and since that day had never let him win again.

"Hey, Lar," Petie called to him now.

"Hey, boy," Larry called back. "Help me with this chain oncet," he said, pulling on what looked like an anchor chain to a steamer out of one of the cars. "I got to oil it up and I can't get it pulled all a way out."

They spent the next fifteen minutes hauling the chain out from the car and spreading it on the ground. "Why you got to oil it?" Petie asked him.

"I don't know. They don't tell you why, they just tell you what."

"Ain't it going to be hard to put it back?"

"I don't need to put it back. I don't know what they going to do with it."

"Looks like it's for a boat."

"I think."

"Well, how to Christ they going to get it on the boat?"

"Hell if I know. Here, raise this part up a while."

When they'd finished coating the links, each the size of Petie's forearm, Larry left the chain in a large coil there in the yard. "I need me a soda now," he said. "I'd rather have me a beer, but I don't drink on the job." Larry was known for only being sober while he was at work. "What you going to do?"

"I don't know. I thought maybe I'd go up the lake, but I don't know."

"Go on if you want," Larry nodded over the yard. "Looks like Number Six is heading out. Getting dark, though."

Petie waited. If he didn't show up tonight at the park, the boys might think he was running away, but it was only about half past four. He was hungry, though.

"You got anything to eat?"

Larry thought a moment. "Hold up. I got some chicken and all." He hobbled over to the conductor's shed just down the yard, and came back with a lunch box. "Here, go head. I had me a dish of spaghetti on Hollins Street when I went out at noon. I forgot I had this, but it's today."

"Okay." Petie took the box, turned toward the train just starting out.

"Bring that lunchbox back, hear me?"

"Yeah. I will. Thanks," he yelled back without turning. He started to trot toward an open car, tossed the lunchbox in and himself after it, his shoulders flying in after his hips the same way he had propelled himself over Catherine's gate before. He retrieved the lunch box, crossed his legs at the edge of the box car, opened the lunch, and raised a chicken leg in salute to an old black man relieving himself under a street lamp across from the train tracks. The man returned the salute with a thin arc of his own business, the drops falling heavy and splattering down, and the man laughed.

Thursday Evening: Goodbye, Goodbye

That mastiff had something to do with everything that happened since then. He'd found it in the rail car. He'd opened the lunch box and then from the far dark corner of the car had heard something, though he'd been sure there wasn't a person in it when he got in. And then the unmistakable snuffle of a dog running its tongue over its nose and swallowing it back in again, and then the dog had stood up and walked over to him, looked at him—looked down at him, actually, because standing it was far taller than the top of his head—and plopped down next to him. He could barely make it out, it was so black, but he could see how big it was and he tried not to feel afraid.

"I ain't got anything for you to eat. This all's mine," he said to it. The dog looked out the car, put its head down on its paws, and seemed instantly to go to sleep.

Petie finished the lunch, threw the chicken bones out, drank some of the coffee, which by now was not particularly hot, and lit a cigarette. He wasn't thinking about anything now. Eventually the signs of Lake Roland coming up began to make themselves known in the shadows, and he looked for a good place to jump. As the train slowed at the approach of an intersection, Petie pushed himself lightly down from the car, his knees buckling a little bit, and his buttocks tapping the dusty ground that sloped away from the train tracks.

"I'll be goddamned," he said to himself, watching the dog look down at him from the car door.

He watched the train cars pass until the last one went by, then climbed up on the tracks and headed back in the direction from which he'd come, toward the lake shore. It wasn't long before he realized that someone was behind him, and he turned, and in the grey saw that it was the dog.

"Well, I'm goddamned," he said again, aloud, and he stopped, and waited for the dog to catch up with him, which, since it was picking its way over the tracks, was taking some time. Petie stepped off the track to the lake side, where the ground was graveled but level, and as he did, the dog stepped off, too, and then came at him at a trot, enormous and black and not a spot of white or brown on that massive face. The dog stopped just in front of Petie, looked at him gravely, as Petie thought—well, he thought, *You look pretty serious for a dog*—and that was all.

"Come up," Petie said, turned and kept walking. The dog's breath was just about on his legs, but he didn't trip him up, and his heels didn't catch at its head.

For another quarter of a mile or so they proceeded this way, sometimes Petie bending over to look at something or pick something up, at which times he felt the dog's breath on his ass, but again, that was all. He had no more idea how a dog that size got down out of that rail car without breaking all its legs than he did how the thing had gotten into the car in the first place. Maybe it was a mountain dog, used to leaping from heights. Maybe it knew to come out sideways. Maybe it had got lucky, and spotted a really flat stretch of ground or road to jump down from. Petie didn't know. Dogs could see better in the dark than people, though, he knew that, and so perhaps that would account for it.

"If you start talkin, then we'll have something to talk about," he said, and threw the piece of flint he had picked up over some bushes and out on to the water. "Jeeze, boy. I'm cold and I need me something to eat." They arrived at the place Petie was looking for, a small path he knew led down to the water and a small stretch of clay he called The Beach. The sun was getting low in the sky and the last light hit the leaves directly, nearly in his eyes when he looked that way.

"You want to go for a swim?" he asked the dog, expecting the thing to at least nod its head. It continued to regard him with that staid and not at all disturbing gravity. "You want something?" he asked it again now, looking down at it like it was a little kid that didn't know how to talk yet. "I ain't got a goddamned thing. I done ate all my lunch, asshole, and I'm still just about to faint with low blood my own self. I don't know what we're going to do." He laughed.

The dog sat down.

"Awright. I'm goin in." By now they were at the beach and Petie started to strip down, but at that the dog growled and stepped in front of him.

"What? You think they got cottonmouths in there, or crocodiles, or something? You think I'm going to drown myself in the dark?"

But the dog would not let him pass. He had heard of this kind of crap on Lassie and Rin-Tin-Tin movies, but had always discounted it, using the apparent lack of intelligence in his own German shepherd as a gauge of what dogs generally were capable of. "They just made it like that," he would say to his friends, meaning the shooting of the film. "It ain't a dog in the universe got that much sense of dedication."

So this had to be something else.

"I told you. I got nothing to eat. You can have my shoes, how bout?" He stooped to pick up one of the shoes he had kicked off, and the dog barked and looked happy all of a sudden. "Okay, Jack, here it is, go get it!" And he flung the shoe out in the direction of the water, but it hit a tree limb and didn't go nearly as far as it should have. He watched it fall into the shallows, where it plopped, filled up, turned on one end, and sank. The dog, naturally, had not moved.

"Well, shit, Jackson. You got more sense than I got, I guess."

He wasn't about to go in after it, though he wouldn't have any money to buy himself anything until a week from next Friday, at least, not to keep himself in Chesterfields and crullers, and he thought again, *Goddamn*. He looked at the dog, standing impassively at sentry, and knew that as little as the dog meant him harm, he would be a fool to try to find out why it didn't want him to go farther down this path or into the water. It was probably cold as a son-of-a-bitch anyway, first thing of April and no sun on the water for the last hour anyway.

"Well, awright. What do you want to do?"

The dog nosed his bent legs, as much as if to say, "Get on back up the road awhile," and Petie laughed again. "Jeeze, boy, you are something else." He stood, turned, and walked back up the path, the dog behind him, and it struck him that far from leading the dog anywhere, he was being followed as a prison guard or policeman follows a man in custody. He knew better than to act scared, or even let himself feel afraid—*One thing I do know, even a stupid dog can smell the fear on you, and who knows what they'll do then*—but he started to look for a getaway on either side of the tracks, a skinny tree, maybe, that he could hang on to until the next train came by and he could jump down over on to it, when the dog trotted out in front of him, barked, and as much as told him to follow, now, double-time.

This is *a goddamned Rin-Tin-Tin picture.* But he ran along behind the dog, the one shoe in his hand in case he needed to bop it on the head, the gravel stones hurting him on the soles of his feet and where they flew up and hit his ankle bones, proceeding this way for another two hundred yards, when the dog ran down into a clearing on the lake side of the tracks and up to a young boy and girl standing in the gloom next to the water.

"Batista!" they shouted as one, flung their arms around his neck, and kissed him madly all over the head that was easily twice as large as either of theirs. As he approached, Petie saw that they were both quite slight, the girl around twelve or so, the boy maybe his age or a year older than himself only. When he got close enough, he could even see that the boy had some respectable stubble on his chin, which Petie knew meant that he had gotten around to the shaving every other day or so stage, and that if he was anything like Petie himself, he enjoyed the scruffy feeling of the whiskers as much as scraping them away with his father's safety razor.

"What you call him?" he said now, and the two looked up, and smiled at him with the self-same smile.

"Did you find him?" the girl asked. "Sometimes he just wanders away while we're swimming and we don't see him, but this time it was hours and hours. We were afraid to go home. It's dark."

The boy, who seemed to have a bit better sense of Petie's measure and had by now taken it, had kept quiet when Petie spoke, but now he said, "We weren't afraid. We just thought he might not be able to find his way back. You know, back to the house. It's kind of far."

Petie smiled at him, the smile that meant that nothing bad was going to happen to anybody as long as he was around, and he saw the boy relax, and return the smile, and then the boy repeated his sister's question: "So, where was he?"

"I come up on the railroad," Petie said, diving deep into his Appalachian tenor, "and this one"—he nodded at Batista like a surveyor taking the size of an edifice by sight—"was in the car. Swear to God. I didn't help him out or nothing, he just come on out and followed me. Wouldn't let me get in the lake, neither, throwed my good shoe in and everything but he wouldn't budge. Then he let me up here and we found you-all. He must be kind of smart, huh?"

They were standing in that light that lets you see everything right before you can't see a thing, and he liked it. "Batista, go get the shoe," the boy said, and to Petie's amazement, the dog trotted off back up to the tracks.

"No, hold up, don't make him do that. I don't think he could get in and get it. It's dark out, man." *Jesus*, he thought to himself, *I must a done wandered into a nut house.*

"He'll come back if he can't," the boy said. And just then Batista did come back, went up to the girl, barked, looked over at Petie, barked again, and left.

"Are you hungry?" the girl asked. "We have some leftover lunch, we didn't eat much of it at all we were so worried. You're welcome to it if you want."

This is getting ridiculous. "Did that dog just tell you I need something to eat?"

"Oh!" she said, looking confused, and then to her brother for guidance, but he was only looking out at the water. "Well, no, he couldn't do that. I mean, he's smart, but he's just a dog after all. He's not mythical or anything. We used to pretend he was, but it turned out he really wasn't after all." The boy turned to her, glaring as Petie supposed, and she stopped in confusion.

He liked the way she spoke. It sort of reminded him of Catherine, but it was softer, more serene, less agitated. He had seen that her hair was blonde and light, and it had given the impression of being nearly see-through, long, going all the way down her back. It looked brown now in the dusk, very like Catherine's. She wore a black band around her head that smoothed over the hairline, and her skin was very thin and he'd also seen a blue cast to it. The boy, by contrast, was as white in his skin, but his hair was just as black as the dog's, and his voice wasn't as sweet as hers, or whatever the boy's equivalent of sweet would be, but it was close. He was not effeminate, but Petie wouldn't have backed him in a fight on the best day he ever had: he was just too skinny and no muscles to speak of whatsoever. He had a little bit of a pot belly, as if he spent most of his time sitting down, and he held his head thrust forward, as if he read a lot and had poor eyesight.

"If you have something you don't want, I could have it," he said to the girl now. "What's your name?"

"Bridget," she answered, bending over something that proved to be a sack and a set of thermoses. She opened one, squinted down into it, smelled it, and smiled. "It's lemonade," she said. "It's really good. My mother made it."

"Shut *up*," her brother hissed then, unaccountably as it seemed to Petie. They had all been talking quietly, as people often do in the gathering darkness, but this sound pierced Petie and he felt sad. However right the boy was not to trust somebody he didn't know, nobody could find something out against you just because you had a mother.

"*You* shut up!" Petie was astonished to hear her say. "She *did* make it, she made it this morning and she gave it to me!" Bridget started to cry, violently, and from where he stood Petie could feel her shaking. As far as he could tell already, she didn't seem to experience anything by halves. "You think she can't do anything but she *can*!"

"Okay. Okay, I'm sorry, she made it. She must have made it. Daddy doesn't know how to make it." The boy kissed the top of Bridget's head, patted her on the shoulder, the way a doctor or a preacher would, Petie thought. *Oh*, he thought then, *oh, I get it*. This guy was like Ronnie, he was that kind of guy, and Petie looked at him with respect.

"It's real good," he said, making his voice deeply warm, "the lemonade. You got a sandwich or something?"

The two looked toward him, once again beautiful in how close they seemed to be to each other, transformed by the obvious pleasure his question had given them, and both said, "Yes!" at the same time. "Can you eat braunschweiger and lettuce and mustard?"

"Just about my favorite," Petie said. "You got any bakery cookies and that's my favorite Saturday supper, as a matter of fact."

"We do!" Bridget looked as happy as if she had been told she would be able to give Petie a new eye or a limb. "We have that kind with the jam in it, and then a couple with the chocolate. But those are really Baker's favorite." Her head turned to her brother and Petie realized this was him.

"They call you Baker?" he asked, trying to keep the surprise out of his voice. "I'm sorry, but I mean, ain't that a last name?"

The boy grunted. "It's really Bakir, but nobody remembers that, and they think you're a snake charmer if they do. Baker's fine."

"So, what's your name, really?" he asked Bridget.

"Oh!" She turned to Baker again. "He's smart!" Turning she said, "It really is Bridget, though. Our father is Benjamin, and our mother is Basima. That means, 'smiling.' Our last name is Belcher, so we are the B Family."

Petie smiled at her, wishing he could see her face better, thinking that, like Catherine, she could go from mature to childish in about a half a second. He thought she must be nearly on fire and he began to feel afraid for her, and in that moment he also stopped loving Catherine for the briefest second, and that made him angry.

Still, he said, as if the giving of his own name would add to everyone's safety, "My name is Peter," dropping the accent. They must have smiled at him, and then turned as one toward the water, where Batista was not seen but heard to be paddling toward the shore, Petie's shoe presumably in its mouth, which, when he got up to the shore it proved to be. He dropped it at Petie's foot.

"Well, I'll be a son-of-a-bitch," he said, laughing, and then they all were laughing, patting Batista as he climbed further up on to the dry land, shrieking when he shrugged the water off his coat, wiping the tears from their eyes.

Petie took them all in, feeling a thing he had, he was sure, never felt in his life. He couldn't name it, didn't have to and didn't want to. "You can call me Petie," he said. "I'm Petie Marlon." He frowned for a minute. "I don't live up here, though," he said, and as if he knew exactly what the problem was, Baker said, "Who cares? We just moved here ourselves anyway."

It was starting to get really dark now, and Petie knew the return train would be coming. He didn't want to leave. Here, although things were very strange compared to what he was used to, there was nothing the matter, nobody making him feel he was a prize or the police. Free, sure. That was it. He was nervous at that thought, enough that Batista looked at him, and barked briefly.

"I got to go," he said, sliding his feet into his shoes, the one dry and bent, the other soaking wet and full of grit.

The other two didn't say anything for a moment, and then Bridget said, "Goodbye. It was very pleasant to meet you." Baker just looked out on to the water again.

Petie didn't know what to say. He was getting angrier by the minute but still didn't understand it, and he knew if it showed that would spoil everything, and he didn't want to spoil any of it.

"Okay," he said instead. "Bye."

As he felt his way up the path to the train tracks, he heard Baker say something sharp, and then in another minute, Batista was flopping alongside him.

"No!" Petie yelled at him. "You go on back, now!"

Batista didn't move.

"I can't take you," he said. "I can't throw a son-of-a-bitching elephant like you up on a rail car. Besides," but he didn't want to finish the thought out loud that Batista belonged with Baker and

Bridget, and not with him. "Aw, shut up," he said, as if the dog had spoken aloud again. "You can't talk, can you?"

Just then the train pulled up, and, seeing Petie wave, some-body slowed it down enough for him to run along until he could grab a rail and pull himself into an open car. He looked out, saw the dog watching as the train pulled away, and he yelled a last time, "Goodbye!" and let the word stretch out like the blare of a train's horn.

Friday Morning: Pause for Paul and Ronnie

Neither of the boys could have said precisely when Paddy wandered away from where they stayed crouched next to Petie after he'd beaten the tar out of him, but it was past midnight. "We just looked up all of a sudden and he was gone," they'd say at the tavern, as if this had been some religious and probably miracu-lous occurrence.

"Let's get eem home," Paul said now.

"We can't take eem home. Don't be ignorant," Ronnie said.

Paul did not dignify this with a reply, but looked down again at Petie, who as far as he could tell was not conscious. "I need a cigarette," he said. He stood, lit up, let the light from the street lamp fall over his tall blond frame, passed his hands over his tiny eyes and sharp, thin nose.

"Christ almighty," he said, blowing smoke. "Jesus Christ almighty."

"Tell you what, let's take eem to my brother Sonny's place, and then we can call the doctor on eem," Ronnie suggested, looking up, the plump hand that had rested over one knee now cupped over his eyes to shield them from the lamplight. He reached over and scratched the shoulder of that arm with the other hand, then passed his palm over his full lips. He looked to Paul like he wanted to get up too but he also looked like he believed if he did, Paddy might rush in from some place to finish the job.

"It's midnight, we can't call the doctor. And Sonny'll bitch us out but good."

"No, he won't. Even if he ain't sleeping one off, either way, he don't like Paddy since he whipped him at the club that one time. He'll think this here was no way to do."

It was no way to do, Paul thought.

It was getting chilly in the wet air. The lamp buzzed louder, it seemed to them both, as if they shared the thought, though neither of them spoke. Paul took a deep drag, let the smoke out through lips flattened over his stuck out lower jaw, flicked his cigarette into the grass with his middle finger off his thumb.

"Okay, let's get eem up."

The boys crouched together, put one arm apiece under Petie's shoulders, tried to lift him. He was huddled to one side, so that on Ronnie's there wasn't much to grab hold of, and the boys' heads nearly touched when they came together. They looked each other in the eye, nodded sharp, heaved. Petie screamed as they lifted his rib cage off the ground, though his eyes stayed closed as if in sleep, not winched together and no frown above them.

The next thing that happened that both boys said until their dying day they were just goddamned about was that they heard a dog growl, very loud and very close by. "Which was crazy," Ronnie said the next day, "because I didn't eem smell him," at which Paul nodded sagely, because everyone knew Ronnie could smell an icicle hanging off a fence in January if a dog had spit on it. They were still holding Petie, whimpering and a trail of blood at the corner of his mouth down onto Ronnie's sleeve and the tears wetting up his arm.

"If it's a dog we got to get him out of here," he whispered to Paul. "Let's just drag him up anyhow."

Paul nodded, they both got as good a purchase with their knees and feet as they could, signaled to go with another nod, and in one motion lifted themselves and Petie up to standing.

"Ah, ah, ah, ah, ah," Petie cried loud, eyes still closed. "Aaaah," he cried, and, "It almost broke our heart," Paul said afterward.

The bark they heard in the next moment came from right behind them and seemed to them to be the precise loudness and pitch of Petie's cry. They turned their heads at the same moment, and there it was, its nose right up against Petie's backside.

"The goddamn thing was big as a pony, all black and this big square goddamn face on him," they said, alternating the story between them.

"Mastiff," Petie would say later that night from the day bed where he smoked and winced every time he pulled on a bottle of Pepsi.

"You keep saying that. Mastiffs are not black anymores. I went up the Enoch Pratt and asked the lady to look it up, and she said no they ain't black, they're brown with *some* black," Ronnie said.

"It was a mastiff," Petie said, and laughed.

They had gotten him home to Sonny's place over on Gilmore, mostly dragging him between them with his arms over their shoulders, trying not to pull on his rib cage too much. It had taken them the better part of three quarters of an hour to get to Sonny's, but they could walk it regular in less than ten minutes. Petie cried nearly the whole time and vomited up blood once, but after that they thought he seemed to quiet down. Getting him up to Sonny's extra bedroom upstairs had just about broken their hearts a second time, because Petie never seemed actually able to pass out all the way, and they knew they were hurting him with every step they took him.

"Why don't we just lay him on Sonny's divan in the living room?" Paul asked as low as he could.

"Because Sonny will kill him if he bleeds on it. If he bleeds in the bed and the doctor had came for him, you know, Sonny won't mind that. He'll understand that," Ronnie said.

"Well, I'ma call the doctor as soon as it gets light out." Paul stopped a minute, hunched up one hip against Petie and tightened his hold around Petie's waist. "Two more steps. Let's do it faster."

They got Petie into the bed in the spare room, and Ronnie had the thought to get a wet rag and wipe his face at least, which he did as Petie lay there with his eyes closed. His arms were straight at his sides, his left knee turned out just a little bit away from the right. He was not pale, but white with a green kind of tinge to his skin ("Like my uncle Bobby just before he passed away from low blood," Ronnie said) and neither of the boys fooled himself into thinking he was asleep. They went back downstairs after a while of standing over the bed and alternately looking down at Petie and over across at each other.

"You want something?" Ronnie asked. "I think it's some scrapple and some eggs."

"No, I don't want nothing, but you go ahead," Paul replied. "I'm ona have a cigarette—wait, listen up, give me a cup of tea— Sonny got Lipton's?"

"Oh, sure, he don't got nothing else. Coming right up."

Paul lit a cigarette, pulled up the shade, looked out at the empty street, ran the phrase "orange pekoe and cut black pekoe tea" through his mind, felt good somehow. He thought he had hardly ever been up at an hour when at least one light wasn't shining through one window down the block. This interested him, he liked it. He sat down in one of the stuffed chairs Sonny had bought from the second hand store on Baltimore Street, a fact which Paul always noted in his mind because Sonny was one of the few people Paul had ever known and certainly the only bachelor he was acquainted with who had paid money for new furniture, even if it had come from a second hand store.

"I'm going to get me some new furniture sometime," he thought now. "I'm going to put some stuffed chairs like this here in my front windows," he thought.

Then he thought that this was the goddamndest night he had ever spent in his life. The dog that had showed up out of nowhere was no stray he'd ever seen and it had been so goddamned big he knew somebody owned it and nobody he had ever heard of had a dog that big in that neighborhood. Petie's German shepherd was the closest dog he knew for size, and everybody talked about that thing all the time, how much walking and running it needed, how much food it had to have, how it was the loudest dog howling when an ambulance or a squad car went by. That fucking pony of a dog must bust somebody's ear drums when it heard a siren, he thought, and, as neither of them could go for very long without running their thoughts by the other, he headed out to the kitchen to ask Ronnie what he had made of the whole thing.

After they'd eaten and drunk and hashed things out, they returned to the living room, where Paul fell asleep in the same chair and Ronnie across the divan. Ronnie woke with a start at about seven in the morning, pulled himself up, ran a hand through his hair. Everything came back to him when he saw Paul passed out, his head askew on the back of the chair in a way Ronnie thought would hurt once he woke up. The house was dead still, and Ronnie thought, *Oh, sugar.*

He got up, went over to Paul, shook his arm softly and tenderly so as not to startle him awake, keeping in mind the presumed stiff neck, and whispered, "Paul?"

Paul came gradually to, stretched out his legs long in front of him, raised his arms over his head, and, Ronnie was relieved to note, smiled as he stuck out his torso and moved his head from side to side. He opened his eyes, seemed to take stock of the environment, smiled up at Ronnie. "Goddamn, boy, how long we been asleep?"

Ronnie pattered out to the kitchen to check the clock on the stove. Paul got up, stretched again, followed him out. "We can call the doctor by now, can't we?" he asked.

"What if he's dead?" Ronnie said.

"The doctor?"

"No, I mean it's so quiet. What if Petie's expired up there?"

"Oh."

"I mean, you know, he could have up and died up there. I wished we hadn't of fell asleep that long. But I don't hardly want to go up and check."

This was not nerves, Paul knew that. The last thing Ronnie needed was the police on him for a dead body. "I don't mind, I'll go on up and check on him," he offered.

"All right. You go up and check on him and then come on back down and we'll see what to do."

A minute later Paul came tapping down the steps almost cheerfully. "He ain't dead," he said. "He don't look too bad, now, neither."

This contribution bucked them both up, and Paul suggested they go down to the call box and try Doctor Agnew, explain to him that there had been a bad fight and they didn't know what to do. They went out the back door, Ronnie jingling his keys and Paul walking fast and happy. They went up the alley, crossed over to Pratt and found the telephone booth, and after a minute of discussion decided Paul was the best one to do the calling.

"He said he'll come on over in an hour," he said.

"He got a hour, Petie?"

"Yeah. Yeah, he does. Let's go up Dolan's and get a couple sodas." They had known a long-necked bottle of Pepsi to cure serious ailment more than once.

Sonny lived one block up from Dolan's store, around the corner on the other side of Pratt and just about three blocks from Petie's house on Stricker. It might as well have been another town in some respects, but Ronnie had grown up over there and Paul didn't mind it. Dolan's was another half block west of Stricker. They peered down Pratt as one, then crossed over on the diagonal as if they'd been downtown. The sun was starting to feel warm, early as it was.

"A soda will taste good right about now," Paul observed.

"Yeah," Ronnie said.

Dolan's heavy door was open, visible only the wooden screen. A good smell, of crullers or cookies, was coming out of it, along with the wood floor, the few raw vegetables, and the boxes of laundry flakes and cakes of bath soap. When they got all the way inside these would be further refreshed by the penny candy display on the front counter, and the hum of the thick green soda cooler where it stood broad and waist-high next to it.

Ronnie reached right over, slid the metal door sideways over the top of the case, and with four fingers pulled out three long-necked soda bottles. Then he reached back in and pulled out a ginger ale.

"In case he don't feel good enough for a soda," he explained.

Seamus Dolan came walking slowly up to the front of the store behind the counter, wiping his hands on the apron he wore. He'd been sorting potatoes.

He looked at Paul with the look that always made Paul feel like he was his fucking girl or something. *Bastard's a faggot*, he thought. He thought of Paddy and what Paddy had done to Petie, and knew he'd enjoy doing something the same to Paddy's uncle. *Except it would be a waste of my breath*, he thought.

He slicked the two sides of his hair back. "Give me a pack of Luckies," he said as rudely as he dared.

"What's the magic word, lad?" Seamus said in his bullshit accent. Even Paddy and his dad didn't talk that thick.

Paul didn't answer. Ronnie had already put twenty cents on the counter for the sodas, and was waiting, curious, at the door. Paul grabbed his Luckies, threw a dime down, turned, and walked out.

"Hold up," he whispered to Ronnie, and then yelled back through the screen, "Nothing you don't have to say to your old lady every night!"

As he knew he wouldn't, Seamus didn't even come out and stand halfway in the door and swear after them down the street. Paul laughed. Then he remembered Petie, and wanted to kill the man again.

Friday Morning: It Was a Mastiff

Petie woke up in Sonny's guest bed just after eight o'clock in the morning, with the doctor over him and Paul and Ronnie hovering at the end of the bed, he wasn't positive what he was doing there or why every part of him hurt more than any part of him ever had before. His face was wet and the doctor was poking him. He knew this doctor, Dr. Agnew, he had come to the Marlon house when Petie's little brother Jimmy had had a really bad case of the mumps the year before. They had thought they were going to lose him, but Dr. Agnew told them what to do, and gave them some medicine out of his bag, and an ice bag they would not have been able to get until Woolworth's opened, and they had followed his directions and given Jimmy the medicine, and stayed up all night to make sure Jimmy's ice bag had enough ice in it, and he had come out of it all right. Petie looked up now at Dr. Agnew's jowls, comfortable and familiar as they hung down from the bones of his face, flat and wide, his skin white and soft with not a bit of stubble showing on the cheeks or the chin, and

Petie could see three short hairs sprouted on the top of his nose. The eyebrows were long and curling, half black and half white. He could see a thread of dried mucus in the wide cavity of one of the doctor's nostrils, and both corners of the doctor's mouth held something stark white, dried, in a spot in the very corner of each side of his mouth. He smelled dark and warm, like a tweed over-coat. Petie wondered how long the doctor had to live, looking like that. He wondered if he would wind up being one of those fifty-six year old men you heard about that just dropped dead, like that. He thought maybe he would, maybe he wouldn't.

"It was a mastiff," he found himself saying. Ronnie and Paul both jumped and looked like they had been shot at through the side window. He didn't know why he had said this, but he knew it must have meant something.

"I don't know what you're talking about, young man, but I'm glad to see you're finally awake," Dr. Agnew smiled down to him. "But you need to sleep, and I'm going to give you a dose, now. It won't hurt, but it will make you feel better and you'll sleep a while more. It won't hurt you."

"Foot, Doc, I ain't afraid of no shot," Petie said. "This ain't bad. I seen worse."

And he remembered later that the doctor smiled and looked satisfied, and said, "I can see that," and then there was all black-ness, and Petie dreamed. He dreamed about Catherine, riding a white horse, a wolf or something like one following beside her, her foot in the stirrup grazing the top of the wolf's back. He dreamed of Dolan getting drunker and drunker and louder and louder at the tavern. He dreamed of Paul and Ronnie, who had changed into rabbits, Paul smoking through the twitching of his lips and nose, and Ronnie placing a bet at the bookie's, his little white paw holding the stub end of a pencil.

He dreamed of his mother, whose body had turned into an enormous orange, pocked with dimples and her breasts covered with little orange tree leaves. He knew about orange trees, he had studied them in school. He dreamed that his father, who was a garage mechanic, had turned into a cat and was working on Catherine's mother's old car, and looking up Catherine's dress because he thought it was the hood of the car. And he dreamed of his dog, Shorty, who it seemed was an alcoholic who spent his evenings drinking bourbon out of a jelly glass and screaming at the tree in the next yard, screaming that the tree was a bitch, that it was a whore, and that he was going to punch the tree in the chest when he got half a chance.

And he dreamed that his own face had turned purple and had swollen in pieces like a head of cauliflower, and that his chest was no longer strong and divided into two perfect muscles, but that it had collapsed and that Catherine was spreading Vicks Vapo-Rub over it, crooning to him while looking at a photograph of Paddy Dolan in a magazine. Paddy was wearing his silks, holding his boxing gloves up before his face, and he was handsome, as handsome a man as Petie had ever seen, and Petie himself was in the corner of the ring, sitting on the three-legged stool and holding a water bucket until Paddy might need it. Petie was short, and thin, and old, and had the chicken-skin neck and grey stubble that all old men had at the end of the day. His arm muscles were gone, and the skin that covered where they once had been hung down in a wrinkled mess, and the same thing had happened to his exposed stomach, and his legs, and his very lips had disappeared, sunk somewhere into his mouth.

And when he woke again he was still in terrible pain everywhere, the room lit up with rays coming in the window sideways, so that he guessed it must be around two o'clock in the afternoon. He needed to go to the bathroom, but when he tried to move it hurt him too much, and he couldn't get his left shoulder to work. He couldn't open his eyes. And then he remembered the night.

Friday: I Could Use a Pepsi Once

When the blow had come from Paddy's bent fist it had taken a long time to make it to Petie's face. He had seen it coming. He had seen it coming, though, for about seven hours, since he had leaned out, sweating and jubilant, on the top of Catherine's back steps pumping that brick and feeling like God almighty. You might have said that it could have been anyone, that Catherine was just an excuse to show off, to play up, to take a chance and give the world what you'd got, to give a sonofabitch like Paddy Dolan what-for and to make sure none of the candy-assed little faggots who hung around him ever questioned you again or got within forty feet of you without shoving his hands in his pockets or offering you a smoke with his eyes averted at a respectful angle away from you, but you would have been entirely wrong. Petie didn't have to prove himself to anyone. He wasn't that kind of man. He honestly didn't give a damn what Paddy or any of these bastards thought. He didn't operate that way. The world was the world and you were a man or you weren't, and if you weren't you followed someone like Petie and did whatever he did. If you were a real panty-waist you followed a piece of garbage like Paddy Dolan and hoped to Christ you didn't spend your life getting the shit kicked out of you by Petie's friends. But Petie didn't waste his time giving you a second thought.

He could not have told you exactly what made him stand up there and challenge Paddy Dolan like that. A word, a stroll up into the invisible circle around Dolan's body that Petie also knew he had and that no one in his life had ever made the mistake of entering uninvited would have done the trick. Even walking away and letting Catherine figure it out for herself would have been possible, acceptable. He didn't think he had ever even said so much as a hello to Dolan before yesterday. But there he was, not like an actor in a movie, not like that, but not like himself, either. And he knew the minute he put his hands on Catherine's back to push her up the steps he was in it, all the way in.

Petie slept, and woke up again, and he was crying now. Every bit of him hurt so bad he couldn't get away from the pain even by thinking of Catherine. His head and mouth were fuzzy. He opened his eyes, found Ronnie standing above him next to the bed, a solicitous look on his face and a bottle of Canada Dry ginger ale in one hand.

"You feeling okay?" Ronnie whispered.

"You got a Pepsi instead?" he answered.

"Yeah, I do!" Ronnie seemed very pleased and hopeful at this. He came back it seemed within the minute with the soda and a pack of cigarettes. "Here you go," he said, holding the bottle out limply.

Petite found he couldn't even hold out his hand to take it. "I got to get up."

"You can't the doctor said."

"But I have to go."

"Oh! Oh, he said use this." Ronnie reached over and then held out a silver thing that seemed to have come out of nowhere and looked like a bean with the top slanted and folded over.

Petie's left arm didn't seem to be working. "I can't pick it up."

"Oh! You got a cast on. Use the other one."

After focusing a moment Petie found his right arm and lifted it up.

"What do you do? You know?"

"I think you just do it."

"Oh."

"You want me to turn around?"

"I don't know. Sure."

He managed to relieve himself without too much confusion or misdirection, most of what spilled landing on him. When he finished, his lower abdomen was a little damp and the shoulder of his left arm was killing him more than it had been, which he would not have thought could have been possible. He tried to keep the tears from coming but it was no good. He could keep from sobbing, though, and he guessed that was something. He said aloud, "What do I do with it?"

Ronnie turned around, looking pleased and somewhat proud of Petie. "Oh!" he said, "I'll take it." And he pattered down the hall and in a second Petie heard the toilet flush.

When Ronnie came back in, Petie said to him, "I want to wash my hand."

"Oh."

Petie couldn't think at all and he worried this might prove to be beyond their corporate powers of disentanglement, but before he could say anything else, Ronnie said, "Do you really have to?"

"Yeah," he said, "I need a cigarette, but I got to wash my hand," he said.

Ronnie seemed impressed by this, as though he hadn't really given the degrees of hygiene much thought previously but was much struck by them. He paused another moment. "Oh! I know what. Lemme get you a washrag once." He again looked very pleased with himself, and went back down to the bathroom.

When he put the washrag in Petie's hand it felt cool and soft. "Hey, could you wipe it on my face once?" he said.

"Sure," Ronnie said. He took the rag, leaned over Petie, and with a tender solicitude that Petie realized you often found on Ronnie's face, carefully wiped it over his eyes, nose and mouth, dabbed it across his cheeks, and pressed it into his forehead. Petie wondered idly where Ronnie had come by this knowledge as it felt tremendously good and also exact in some way he could not have put words to.

"You want me to wipe your belly and all, too?"

He thought idly that after this he might have to kill Ronnie or at least beat the shit out of him, but he nodded.

"Give me a cigarette. What did you get?"

"Camels."

"Camels. I been wanting me a Camel since I don't know what."

"You want me to light it for you?"

"Jesus, asshole, what are you, my mother? I got a hand, it's why I washed it, for Christ's sake. Just light me up a match once before I beat your face in." This speech felt good but exhausted him, and he sunk back further into the pillow.

And at this Ronnie winced with a look Petie couldn't untangle. "Sorry, man."

"All right," he whispered back. Ronnie held the match to the tip of the cigarette, and Petie drew in deeply. The cigarette tasted sublime. Maybe he wouldn't have to kill Ronnie after all. A Lucky wouldn't have tasted this good, that was for damned sure. Sometimes, and you never knew when, Ronnie really had a head on his shoulders. "Where's Paul?" he asked.

"Oh! Well, the doctor said if you woke up and you wanted to eat something you could, so he went over to get us some subs and another soda."

"He getting mayonnaise on mine?"

"Shoot, yeah. When did you ever eat a sub without it was no mayonnaise on it? Shoot!"

Petie laughed and then took a drag of smoke, closed his eyes, let the smoke trail slowly out of his nostrils. He started coughing. A little blood came up, and he wiped his mouth with the side of his arm. He heard Ronnie sit down in the chair, and he was glad not to be alone, but he didn't open his eyes and Ronnie seemed to know better than to talk anymore.

"Goodbye," he muttered from the bed with his eyes closed, and Ronnie looked up quickly, sharp, lit another cigarette for himself, and took another swallow of soda.

Saturday Afternoon: Bellemore

How they had managed to get him off the lake and up on to their porch Petie was never quite willing afterward to recall. He thought if one more person witnessed him crying with the tears coming down his face he didn't know what he'd do. It was a good thing he couldn't hit anybody yet, that was all he knew.

They'd had to leave Mr. Emerson behind on the beach, and Petie recalled the look on his face as he waved goodbye, happy and wistful. He said he'd get on Teddy's train, that he might explore a while, or he might just stay there or whatever it might be, but not to worry themselves about it, and that was the last Petie thought of him. And then they were in the boat, and that had been peaceful and painful, and then they had gotten out, and that had only been painful, and after Baker called his father, who from whatever hospital he was working at had called a taxi for them, they had taken him to their home.

Bellemore Road. What a bullshit name for a place to live, he thought now, and the unfriendliness of the thought displaced his bodily pain for a moment. He wondered if he would ever feel better again. *Stricker, Pratt, Lombard. I'm going to live me and die on Stricker Street*, he thought, and then began to sing "Bad, Bad Bellemore" under his breath. He had nearly pleaded with them to leave him here on the porch, but there he was now so cold he began to think he was going to die of exposure.

He looked around the front lawn. Baker had said they weren't from around here. Petie didn't think anybody could actually be from around this place, but it might be the kind of place somebody might like to move to, eventually, when they were old and had grandchildren, but right now he was so damned cold he couldn't give a half a care. The porch itself wrapped around the frame house big as a boardwalk, he supposed. There were a few chairs made out of something like he didn't know what — not wood and not rope. He'd seen it before but he didn't know what you called it. A couple of empty plant pot stands in wrought iron were collected over in one corner, and the lawn of the house spread out in he guessed about a half an acre before the road, with plenty of trees he didn't know the names of, and a tall hedge blocking the road itself. The sidewalk wasn't cement, but made out of slate slabs, uneven and filled in with gravel or some kind of small stones. Petie bet it would be hell in the winter. His teeth began to chatter hard.

Bridget and Baker came out of the house loaded up with a tray that they set carefully down next to him, and the unbearably welcome sight of two unfiltered Pall Malls and a stainless steel lighter met him. He reached for one, and shivered. There was some food, crackers and meat, and a glass of milk, which they'd have to kill him to get him to drink that.

"Petie, you're really cold," said Baker. "You should come inside."

"No, I'm fine," he said, his teeth chattering so that he could barely hold the cigarette in his lips. He flicked the lighter open and lit up, drawing the first drag of smoke in like pure oxygen, and it warmed him nearly all over. "But, you know, if you got a blanket."

"Get him a blanket, Baker!" Bridget snapped.

"Okay, okay, I was going to. Jeeze Louise," Baker muttered.

"Sometimes he doesn't have any idea about anything at all. What about coffee? Except I don't know how to make it."

"No, thanks, I don't really like it all that much," Petie said, and didn't add *when you don't know how to make it*. "Maybe if you got some of that nice lemonade again?" But Bridget looked then like she might start crying, and he was irritated by this, and tried to cover it up. "So, Bellemore, huh?" he said. "Where you all go to school at?"

She looked a little better then, and he thought once again how quickly her mood could change. "We go to Friends. It's not too far from the hospital. We go in the car with our father, it's not too hard."

"Huh. I went to Poly for two years," he lied. "It was all right. I took the bus. Your mother work?"

"No. Does yours?"

"Sure. She's a cocktail waitress. Couple nights a week, you know."

"Oh! That must be interesting. I'd like to do that."

"You? Oh, sure. Well, maybe after you've growed up some, went to high school."

"Oh, yes!" She giggled. "Nobody would hire a cocktail waitress that still had to wear saddle shoes." She laughed, then paused. "Petie?"

He tried to shift where he sat, and was shot through with the pain again. "Huh?"

"Can I come see you at your house some time?"

"I don't know. Maybe." He took a drag on his cigarette, let out a stream of smoke, suddenly wanted nothing more than to be left alone, but she didn't understand the way she seemed to have yesterday, and she didn't move.

"Please?"

Why wouldn't she stop bothering him? "Hey, don't bug me about it. I said maybe."

He looked over and saw that her lips trembled hard as she worked to keep her face still, and that in a moment she was going to cry, and it immediately enraged him, that he wanted to slap her.

"Jesus, is that all you can do?" he flung at her. "Cry, cry, cry, *oh, oh, oh*! Damn. You get on my nerves, girl. Go on, Jesus."

She stayed where she was. Her chest beat forward and back, and she gulped on sobs she wouldn't let out. He hated her and loved her at once.

"Hey. Hey, kid," he said. "I'm sorry. Come on. Don't mind me." He wanted to reach out a hand to her, put his arm around her, and wanted to get up and run out. Well, maybe he would never run again. Damn her. He didn't understand her and he wanted to, but he couldn't, and he couldn't stand those two things together for another second, and he could not keep his temper, and yelled at her again.

"Go on! Get back in the house if you can't do something else but cry all over me," he cried. "Ain't somebody supposed to be bringing me a blanket or something, for Christ's sake?"

He thought of every word he could say to her, and a few he knew he couldn't, but he couldn't bring himself to say any of them and he began to cry like a baby again himself, and inside of himself he swore vengeance on Paddy Dolan, and Lake Roland, and these goddamned Bakers, and this goddamned street he had to get off of but soon.

Then Baker came out and Bridget, as though all she had been waiting for was that Petie would not be left alone, ran past him and tumbled into the house in the exact same way she had tumbled out of the boat and over to Petie on the shore, where he had taken one look at her translucent hair and skin and known for a certain fact that though he had sacrificed nearly his own life to see her this day, he could no more be with her than fly to the moon. He had never desired to see another human being before in his life, and knew that he would never be able to see her again after this if he wanted to stay alive. It wasn't like Catherine. Catherine he could handle. This was something else. He would have to fake it.

"What happened?" Baker said, where Petie would have asked, "What's the matter with her?" Baker was danger, too, but Petie knew how to deal with his kind.

"Nothing," Petie said. "Give it over, I'm freezing to death," motioning to the blanket, but Baker put it around him, and handed him some woolen gloves. "If you need them," he said.

"Sure," Petie said, and tossed them aside. "Listen, you got a beer?"

"Yes, I think so. But I don't think you should."

Petie winced. Ronnie would not have said that. "Just don't worry about what I should do," he said, his eyes closed. "I need me a couple more cigarettes, too."

He opened his eyes then, picked up the second one from the tray, lit it, breathed in the smoke, closed his eyes, let the smoke trail out of his nostrils just the way he did at the ball park. When he opened his eyes again, Baker was looking at him with that irritated, sad look he seemed to have on most of the time, when he wasn't reassuring Bridget about something or smiling with her like a jackass over something else.

"What are you looking at?" Petie flung at him.

"Nothing," Baker said, but he really meant it, and so Petie couldn't really get mad about it, and that made him angrier. *Mountain out of a molehill*, he thought, except that now he was also beginning to worry from how his body felt that something else might be wrong with him that wasn't any molehill. He took another drag, coughed a bit, wiped his mouth, and there was another small streak of red blood in the spit.

Saturday Evening: This Ain't Bad, I Seen Worse

Baker went back into the house, and Petie could hear a high voice and then the door creaked again, and a dark-haired woman in her forties stepped out.

"Good afternoon," she said. "I'm Mrs. Belcher. How can I help you?"

Then there was the sound of gravel and a car pulled into the lane next to the house, and Petie saw a man in a new Studebaker drive down it and pull around to the back. He heaved himself to his feet by the bannister, swearing under his breath. He threw the cigarette out on to the lawn and turned to the woman.

"My husband," she said to him as if he had asked, and she, too, ran into the house, slamming the screen behind her.

Petie stared after her, coughed, and spat. He wanted to sit down again and found he couldn't, but standing seemed to be all right, and he was breathing easier, too. In just a few moments, the door opened again, and Baker, Bridget, and the man from the car came out.

"Dad, this is Peter," Baker said, and the man extended his hand.

"Pleasure," he said, "Welcome. I see you've gotten yourself into a bit of a mess," chuckling exactly like Dr. Agnew, who he in some measure resembled, though he was very thin and about fifteen years younger.

Petie shook his hand with his right, said, "Hello," but that was all. Dr. Belcher seemed to be looking him over without looking like he was, but he finally said, "Would you mind if I just checked a few things? I promise not to hurt you, but you might have a few ribs broken and it wouldn't be a bad idea just to see."

"No, sir, that's all right. I seen the doctor already, and he wrapped me up pretty good."

"How bad does it hurt?"

"Oh, nothing, really," Petie lied. "It ain't too bad. If I could just get me a cab and go home, that's all. I didn't mean to be no trouble."

"No, no, it's no trouble. It's just that I think your doctor might have missed something that he'd check again himself if he were here and looking at you. If there's something else the matter, I don't think a long cab ride would do you any good, either."

His voice was professional and compelling, and Petie felt afraid then for the first time since Paddy first hit him.

"Well, all right, sir, if you say so. You're the doc." He tried to laugh, and coughed and wheezed, and Baker and his father moved forward with Petie between them while Bridget held the door open.

"We'll just come right inside here to my office," which proved to be a room off a hall that could easily have held the front rooms of Petie and Catherine's houses, and that Petie instantly hated. The office was small and nice, though, and it reminded him of Dr. Agnew's. There were plants in the windows and a vase of hot-house flowers on a coffee table flanked by padded straight chairs, and next to the large wood desk there was a doctor's examination table where Petie was lifted up.

His legs hurt where they dangled off the table, and he slumped, and his chest pained him so he sat up straighter, and that was better but not much. "I forget your name," he said, and then just saying that much seemed to take all of the energy he had left. He wanted to lie down, to be left alone.

"Dr. Belcher."

"Oh, yeah. You're like a stomach disease doctor, ain't you, ha ha." He nearly whispered this, and closed his eyes again.

"Yes," Dr. Belcher said without laughing, "that's right, that's a good one. But I'm going to listen to your chest now, so be still and don't talk."

He put the cold end of the stethoscope to the bandages on Petie's chest, then felt with very light hands all around his ribs.

"Okay," he said finally. "That's fine. You don't sound like any-thing really bad is the matter, but if you're going to get better, you need to stay put, at least for the next twenty-four hours. I wish you'd stay here for the night, or let me put you in the hospital. And you need to stop smoking for a day or two."

"No, sir, I'm fine. I can smoke, it don't hurt at all." Petie pan-icked at the idea of no cigarettes.

"Maybe not, but my guess is that though your lungs aren't punctured, they are bruised, and that's serious business. They need to heal and rest up along with the rest of you."

"Well, I ain't going in no hospital." He wasn't even sure if you had to pay for the hospital, but pay or no, he wasn't going in one unless it was do or die, and if he hadn't died already, once more wasn't going kill him.

"Then let me get you up to bed. You can't take another long car ride. I wish I had a bed downstairs here to put you in. How did you get to the house in the first place?"

"I come up on the railroad, I had somebody, he helped me."

"But there's no train that stops here." Petie didn't reply, and apparently Mr. Belcher thought better of pressing him. "Well, would you like me to call your home for you?"

"Sure," he said, "if I'm staying, and I guess I'm staying," and then, "I'll have to give you somebody's number," and gave him Ronnie's to get the message to his folks he'd be back, "Tomorrow," he said as positively as he could.

They made the call and Ronnie faithfully swore that the next thing he would do would be to walk up and get the message to whoever was home at Petie's. After protesting Dr. Belcher's assurance into the mouthpiece that he wouldn't be needing any sodas or cigarettes, Petie seemed to have nothing left, and the doctor took him in his arms and carried him bodily upstairs to a good-sized bedroom whose bed faced a massive bay win-dow overlooking the back yard, which, after he'd asked if they couldn't push the bed right up to the glass, he saw was twice as deep as the front and ended in what appeared to be a woods with the sun going down behind it, and, *Son-of-a-bitch*, there was that goddamned Batista asleep with its head on its paws like a regular dog out there in the grass, with the dew gathering all over him, probably.

"Do you want him to come up?" Bridget asked as her father settled him pretty nearly painlessly into the bed, arranging the pillows and covers for him as comfortably as he had ever had them, even at home. She had waited outside the office door with Baker once the exam started, and both of them had followed silently up the stairs. Petie then noticed that, quite other than how the girl and boy had been at the lake, nobody in this house seemed to talk any more than they absolutely had to. The quiet generally was driving him nuts, but worse, he was goddamned good and tired of her seeming to know exactly what he was thinking, getting inside of him where she had no business being, and, no, he didn't care for that goddamned dog in the room with him, and he said so.

"Watch your language, son," Dr. Belcher said, and as this was not anything more than his own father would have said, he didn't get mad, but didn't apologize, either.

"Can I eat?" he asked then, as if they had gone to the hospital after all.

"Yes, I'll—I'll ask my wife to put a tray together for you. Bridget, why don't you help?"

Bridget lowered her head and didn't reply, following the doctor out of the room.

Baker asked if he wanted anything else, and he said, "I don't know, man. You got any playing cards?"

"No. Do you want a book?"

This Baker was the end, Petie decided. "Jesus, man, what would I want with a book? You got some perfume for me, too?" He knew it was the pain, he didn't want to talk this way to Baker, but he couldn't help himself.

Baker didn't answer, looking out the window in the way that had made Petie want to hit him since they had gotten to the house. It was like Catherine's steps, he thought, it was the god-damned house, he bet, that was changing him, putting him out of temper, or maybe it was the other way, it was making him softer and making him care about things that put this fury into him. It wasn't right to care so much about things that weren't worth caring about.

"Jesus Christ," he spit out, "don't you ever stand up for yourself? Pussy!" but the last word he muttered only and he didn't think Baker heard it.

"What would I be standing up for?" Baker said without any apparent feeling at all. And then he did stand, moved the chair away, pulled a table up to Petie's bedside, and walked away.

Saturday Night: Bravely and Well

"Yeah, go home and cry, baby," Petie said into the air, and collapsed again, weak as an alley cat. *You get 'em in the alleys*, he said to himself.

"My son's not a baby," a woman's voice said then. "He's strong and noble, so strong. Please, it won't be liked if you speak that way to him."

She came over to the chair, pulled it closer to the bed again, sat down. He noted again that she was dark, with heavy features in a puffy face, but that otherwise she was fairly trim. She was not holding a tray full of anything to eat, though, that was for sure.

"He fought very bravely and well, that's what they told us," she said, and relapsed into silence, but didn't move. Bridget finally brought up some very good soup with beef and carrots in it, some orange juice, and something like a platter full of jello with fruit cocktail on the bottom, and then she went out again. Once he was finished, Petie definitely wanted a soda and a ciga-rette. He and Mrs. Belcher sat in the near darkness. A small lamp was on behind them, but the light hurt Petie's eyes, and they put on just enough for him to see to eat, and Mrs. Belcher had stayed and shooed everyone else out of the room. He refused her offer to help him eat, but when she asked if he could stay, he had said, "Yes ma'am, suit yourself," and she did.

Bravely and well was what they always said, and she said it again, and now that he was rested it sounded right, so he grunted, and she seemed to take that for interest, and began to speak.

"We're not from here, you know. My people come from upstate New York, practically at the top of the world. We came over from Turkey, as a matter of fact, when I was about twelve years old. My father was a doctor, too, and I went to college, but that wasn't liked, not by some of my relatives. And then I got engaged, and that wasn't liked, either. And then I met Dr. Belcher, and he was a good man, he seemed to be a very good man, I thought, but it still wasn't liked."

She reached into her sweater pocket and said, "Would you like a cigarette?"

"Hell, yeah," Petie said. "Sorry—I mean, yes, ma'am, I been wanting one for a couple hours now."

"Oh, my. I'm so sorry, I don't know why you weren't offered one before, but please." She handed him the pack, Kools, which he never smoked, but something was better than nothing. He took one, handed it back over, but she said, "Keep them, please, you may need them in the night. I don't smoke at night myself. It's not liked."

The menthol burned in his mouth and made his lungs feel like raw peppermint, but the smoke was good, and just having the thing in his hand was a relief. "So what about Baker?" he said. "What all happened?"

"Oh. I don't—well, I don't really remember all of it. I just remember the letter, for the most part. They said he died very bravely, that he kept quite a number of the others from being killed. That's a good deal to be proud of."

Oh, boy, Petie thought, *she's nuts.* "So, when did he join up and all?"

"It would have been right after Pearl Harbor, I think, just at the start of 1942." That would have made Baker six or so, and made whoever she was talking about fifteen years older than him, maybe a little bit less.

"After that," she went on, "I don't know. I live here with Dr. Belcher and his children, but my son — I miss him more than anything. It wasn't really liked when I cried about it at the time, so I don't really talk to anyone about it. But there was something," she turned to Petie, "something about your face, and what Dr. Belcher's daughter said about you, that I thought I might just visit with you a little bit. I couldn't visit with him, you see, and now that you've been wounded, well, I thought perhaps that might make up for things."

Petie had thought this lady was Baker and Bridget's mother. Now he wasn't sure, but Dr. Belcher had certainly referred to her as his wife. He tamped out the cigarette in the empty jello bowl and lit a second. "So, you went to college, huh?" he said. He was getting tired and wanted to close his eyes, but thought if he kept her talking he could just lie there and smoke a while and rest, but he was getting nervous, too.

"Oh, yes. I was going to be a nurse. I did love the nursing classes. But then I met Dr. Belcher...no, that's not right. I met another man. I don't remember his name. I don't think we married, but I'm not certain of it. He was very much not liked, and I do recall that my father even struck him once when he came to the door. And then my little brother was born, you know how that is, and he was a charming little thing. I took him with me when Dr. Belcher and I were married. I don't really know what happened to him. I think eventually he must have gone back to my parents.

"And then Baker was born, and we were so happy. He was the happiest baby, with black hair all over his head, and then it fell out and grew in so blonde, you would have laughed to see it! Oh, he was delightful. And then," she said, folding her hands over and over as if they worried her, "they said he had to enlist, that everyone had to enlist. And I just didn't understand it. But he was very brave, so they said. I don't know how it could have been liked, but that's exactly how it happened."

She stood, and moved over to Petie, and sat down sideways on the edge of his bed, reached out her hand, and lightly touched his face and the bandage on his head. He tried not to flinch, or to burn her with the cigarette she was now leaning close to. She smelled lovely, like the menthol and the tobacco, and some perfume he would not have thought he would like, but smelling it would never forget.

"What's that perfume you've got on?" he asked, like an idiot.

"I don't know. I don't remember," she said. "It was a gift. Do you like it?"

"Yes," he said. He thought she was going to kiss him, and that if she did, he was going to burn her stomach with the damned cigarette. "Excuse me, ma'am, let me just get rid of this," he said, and she leaned back again.

"Oh! I'm so sorry! I didn't realize you were smoking. I think I had just come in to check the bedpan. Do you know where it is?" This was—man, he wasn't ever going to forget this, and was he going to razz Baker about it.

"Um, no, I, uh—I think they must have took it out previously." He was trying not to laugh but he couldn't keep his mouth closed.

"Oh! Well. Can I get you anything, then?"

"No, ma'am, I think I got everything, unless there's a soda or a beer or something." He thought he had a good chance of getting those out of her now, anyway.

"Oh, certainly, I'll ask." And then she did lean over, and stared at him full in the eyes, which he would remember as being in some way more thrilling than any kiss would have been. She straightened, smoothed the covers with her hand as efficiently as a nurse might do, and turned to leave.

"Oh!" she said—the mannerism from her didn't annoy him in the slightest—"here is a visitor for you! Isn't that nice? Don't be too long, now," she said as Bridget and Baker became visible. "The patient needs his rest if he's going to rejoin his unit." And she laughed what Petie thought was a chirpy little nurse's laugh.

Neither of the children smiled. "Mother, Father asked for you, if you'd meet him in the dining room for a little supper," Baker said to her.

She stared at him for a long moment, and then seemed to come back to herself.

"Oh! Why, thank you darling," Mrs. Belcher replied, to Petie's amazement. "I'll go right down. We all know how he dislikes eating alone. I wonder what we're having." She trailed out of the room, and as she left Petie burst out laughing.

Saturday Night: It's Joy

Neither of the children laughed, or even smiled, Bridget's head was hung down nearly into her chest.

"What were you talking about?" Baker said.

"Oh, nothing much," Petie lied. "I like her. What's that perfume she wears?"

"It's called 'Joy,'" Bridget said, looking up at him.

"Huh," Petie answered. "It's nice."

Bridget sat on the edge of the bed, lightly, and held out her wrist for Petie to smell. "It is. I sneak a drop on nearly every day. It reminds me of her."

Baker was standing as he did, staring out of the window.

"So, the dog sleep outside at night?" Petie asked.

"No," Baker said without turning, just as he had done at Lake Roland. "When we can find him, he sleeps in the basement or in Bridget's room. He's not supposed to do that, but she cheats and lets him. But many nights these days we can't find him, and he's not in tonight. He'll come home, though. He seems to know his way around by now."

"So what do you all do at night?"

"We play Monopoly or do the cross-word puzzle." This from Bridget, who was still sitting on the bed exactly like a visitor in a hospital room. Baker had gone off to see about the soda or the beer, and had promised to bring one or both of them up to Petie without fail.

"You do what?"

"Well, that's what we do. We aren't allowed to listen to the radio, and we don't have a television set because the black and white pictures distress my mother too greatly."

For the umpteenth time Petie reflected that these people beat all and he didn't know what. He was feeling more himself by the minute.

"Have they gone to bed already?"

"Mother probably has, if they've finished eating. Father is usually up late, in his office, working on research and reading and so forth. He works nearly all the time."

Petie waited for a moment, then said, "Your mother thinks Baker was in the army or something, don't she? But he ain't that old, is he?

"No, he's not," she whispered. "It was my uncle, my mother's younger brother, Robert." She flicked her fingernail on a ledge of the chenille bedspread. "He was killed in action. I don't even know where. I was very little when it happened and I don't remember him, except that he was going to be married, and now we don't even ever get to see his fiancée, or talk about her—she doesn't want to see us or my grandparents. For some reason he lived with my mother and father, and Baker was just like his little brother. I was only the baby. I guess I'm still the baby."

Petie didn't know what to say to this. "So your mother is a little bit off her rocker, then, huh?"

"Yes. Yes, I guess that's right. She comes in and out of it, almost every day. She does quite a bit around the house, and she has her friends, but they are never allowed to come here, and she and Father don't even speak. It's not Father's fault. She blames him, but Baker said he did everything he could to try to make everything better, but she just can't see it. We didn't even mind not bringing you in the house at first because she can't stand anybody coming to the door. And every now and then she'll have a very hard time and will have to go into the hospital for a while. But she did make that lemonade yesterday. And she talked to you."

"Yeah, well." Petie couldn't think of anything else to say. "Huh. That must be something, I mean, to live with, something like that."

Bridget stood up, clenched her fists. "She is my *mother*. How can you speak about her that way? Didn't you listen to her? Didn't you like her? Don't you even care about *anything*? Don't you even *care*?"

She dashed more tears away, but Petie had had it, full up to here. Whatever it was that he had wanted from her, from all of them, was done with. He didn't know why he couldn't care about her mother being crazy—but he did like her, he had proved that when he talked to her, hadn't he? Jesus Christ, the woman wasn't *his* mother—he didn't even know these people, any of them. He hadn't asked them to come by for him, had he? No, sir, he had not. He had just been there, and they had just shown up. That was all it was.

It was them, the kids, that he had come not to like, and he didn't know why, he had thought that he liked them better than anybody he had ever met, but it turned out wrong. Maybe it was the pain, he thought for a second, but then he knew that wasn't it. He didn't know why he hated this house of theirs, either—it wasn't that they were rich, it wasn't that, he planned to be rich someday himself, playing baseball or working on the railroad or something. It was how stupid-ass sad they all had turned out to be underneath all those bright looks and feelings, how common they were when they had seemed to be so different, but most of all how much they thought about every little goddamned thing and then felt like they had to either bottle it up until it choked them, or talk about it until everybody was blue in the face, and they never picked the right one to do.

And the other truth was they were showing him something, something about how angry he was that it seemed like wherever he went he was starting to turn into another person. But he was goddamn sonofabitch not going to keep being the person he turned into when he was around them. He would never survive it—no beating he could stand still for would compare next to it.

And right after that he felt like he couldn't get his air, and he was down on the ground, curled up, Paddy Dolan hammering away at him, it was like he was right there, after he had seen that goddamned dog but before he had had to wake up and remember it all.

He took a couple of breaths, and the feeling calmed down, and he was in the room again. *Aw, bullcrap*, he said to himself but loud, and that made him come all the way back to himself. They were hovering over him, he found, and he swore at them, and they both leaned away as if to avoid his fists. Who in hell did they think they were, anyway—who the hell did they think they were going to *be*? Didn't they even ever think about that?

He breathed deeply some more, reached under the pillow and pulled out the cigarette pack and the matches, lit one deliberately, blew out the match in the direction of Bridget's face, and tossed the match on the floor. She jumped up to stamp on it, and then picked it up and looked at it.

"I'll get you an ashtray," she said.

"Yeah," he said. "You go head and you do that."

She looked at him for a long moment, not as her mother had but in a way much older than her mother. He knew he wouldn't remember a lot of things, but he'd remember that look for a long time, maybe forever. She turned and went out without speaking again, and Baker followed her, wordlessly as well.

Saturday, Late: You'll Have to Forgive Us

And it was not Bridget but her mother who came back in a few minutes later, carrying another tray with all the implements of smoking including a long black and white cigarette holder which Petie was nearly tempted to try out when he saw it, along with a bottle of soda, a bottle of beer, two glasses, and a dish of what looked like strawberry ice cream.

"I'm sorry," she said. "Bridget has a case of the nerves ever since we lost my brother. She cries and cries. You'll have to forgive her, but she's been in and out of institutions and we're not quite sure if she'll ever get any better." She sighed, and looked sadly down at Petie, then seemed to brighten. "I'm looking forward to tomorrow," she said, and paused to fill one glass with beer and the other with soda. She looked like anybody's mother sitting down to a nice talk with one of her friends. "What's your pleasure?"

"Jeeze, uh, I'll take the soda," Petie said, not knowing now which end was up and which, not down but beginning to consider whatever the opposite of up would now be, and how long it would take him to break out of this place in the morning. "I'll take one of them Pall Malls, too, if you don't care."

"Help yourself," Mrs. Belcher said. "I'm so looking forward to tomorrow. You should get your rest in a moment, but tomorrow we'll have to have a nice long talk, and you can tell me all about everything."

And they sat and smoked like friends of long standing, and Petie drank both from the soda and from the beer, and even sloshed down some of the melted ice cream. When he finally fell asleep he stayed that way, but for one visit from Dr. Belcher during the night, and when he woke then she was still there with him, sitting in the chair.

But Sunday wouldn't be like she had said at all. She got up without speaking and went out right after he woke, and he was alone in that room, and he would not see her, or the children, or the father at all that day. It would be quiet, nobody but him and some maid lady in the house who kept bringing him things to eat and drink, him sitting around first in the bedroom, then downstairs in this library room they had, not reading, kicking his heels against the chair legs, being hungry even though he'd just eaten, wanting to smoke. It wouldn't be any of the things that he feared it would be, and none of the things that as he fell asleep he imagined and wished it would. It wouldn't be what he would even know how to take, and he would be speechless and static in the face of it, all day long, and after the maid put him in a cab and sent him home, and for years and years after.

Part Five: Catherine.

Thursday, Early Morning: So Pretty

On Stricker Street, Catherine Bernstein lay in her bed and looked at the wall that divided her house from Petie's. Neither knows it, but each wakes nearly every morning and thinks of the other for a while before getting up. Petie has a pair of girl's glasses on his dresser found on the banks of Lake Roland, which he often used this time to consider: the girl who lost them, who she had been, how poorly she must have been able to see that she couldn't find the glasses after she dropped them, and how he wished Catherine wore glasses so that he could give these to her—not as a gift, of course, but *You know*, he'd say to her, to have on hand. Petie always woke up at six, regardless, and looked at the glasses, and thought about how they would look on Catherine's solemn and narrow face.

Catherine thought, *Petie lives next door to me. I love him.*

She turned her head to the window and watched needles of sun slice their way into the house. That spring she turned thirteen and knew that she loved him. They had lived next door to each other most of their lives, but before this year she had not given him a thought.

Petie swings cats in people's doorways, she began again, feeling him next to her through the wall.

He spoke like a trapper in Appalachia though he'd never seen a bit of nature bigger than the baseball diamond at Carroll Park in his life. She imagined him whirling ginger fur on the end of a piece of rope, the same he taught her to braid into belts and bracelets and fancy shoelaces. She secretly collected the bits of rope he forgot to take with him and kept them under her bed in a Dutch Masters cigar box. She suspected somehow the rope and the cats were connected. But what if you got into trouble?

"Oh, I wouldn't," he said. "I'd be runnin so hard they wouldn't eem'n see me. I'd just whip that cat around by the tail (Oh, by the *tail*, she thought) and hurt em good right in the front of their face. But I don't do it to just anybody. You got to make me mad first, you got to play with me."

She would never play with Petie. She was set on getting him—at thirteen she knew that much—and she knew he was set on pretending he didn't know she was. That's what she thought, anyway. But she also thought that if she looked up at him just right the next time she saw him, he'd know she wasn't playing with him, and that would be all right.

I love you, Petie, she said to herself again. *I love you.*

Even at thirteen, though, sometimes issues of compatibility occur to a person, and just the night before she asked her mother if she thought Petie was trash. They stood in the kitchen before the back window, where she could see him chasing his German shepherd around the small square of cement that was his back yard. He looked demented, his expression, she thought. He was holding something long and thin and red-colored up to the dog to bite at, and each time the dog jumped, Petie would yank the thing away and punch the dog hard in the chest. It would yelp, but keep coming back to get whatever it was that Petie was taunting it with. Both knees of Petie's trousers were ripped across as if someone had slashed them with something a couple of times apiece, and where his tee shirt wasn't yellow with age it was grey with dirt.

"Don't say trash, honey. No, he's not, at least, not yet."

The last was said mostly under her breath. Catherine wondered what she meant. She hadn't asked exactly what she meant, but if they had been able to talk about it, they would have said Petie's father and mother weren't trashy, they had jobs and were well-spoken and that was still pretty good to go by in their neighborhood if you needed something. Petie's father went out in the country and hunted squirrel and possum and such, but a lot of men she knew did that. His mother was one of those ladies who got her hair done in a cocoon of orange yellow, crusted over with hair dressing, and she wore bright red lipstick and nail polish, but there was nothing unrespectable about her. Catherine always thought Petie looked as if his mother had been a toothless old woman in a dirty apron and grey bun smoking a corncob pipe, rocking her life away on the porch of a shack in West Virginia.

The day he told her about the cats she had also gone straight to her mother.

"Well," she said, "is it wrong if you kill an animal? Like an alley cat or something?"

"Depends on the animal. I guess there are enough alley cats in the world that God wouldn't miss a couple."

Catherine was relieved. She wouldn't have cared if she thought Petie was doing something wrong, though. She admired his cat-slaughtering skills on principle.

It was also true that her mother didn't outright approve of her hanging around Petie or listening to his stories, so she mostly had to try to be near him while her mother was at work, in the fur department at Hutzler's, where Catherine would visit her most Saturdays on her half-days, and then they would go across the street to the drugstore and get club sandwiches at the soda fountain, with a milkshake for Catherine and a cup of coffee for her mother. Even so, Catherine could still never imagine how any one store could have enough furs in it to support the livelihood of a whole person, but Petie said he guessed it was because of all the big-game hunters he claimed they still had in those days.

"Yessir, you get you one of them leopards or tigers or something, and somebody got to clean it and scrape the fur off the outside and everything," he mused.

She told him she hoped he wasn't suggesting her mother cleaned out dead leopards.

"Oh, no, they do that before, but then they got to sell it to a rich lady and she don't get to wear it but for a coupla months around Christmas and New Year's. All the rest of the time they have to keep em clean so they don't disintergrate and all."

She asked her mother about this, too, and she said it was pretty close.

Catherine had thought she should go out and interrupt Petie and get him to stop tormenting that dog, but Petie never came when she wanted him to. He would have just kept it up with the dog, staring at her, that demented look and laugh on his face, and he wouldn't stop.

Even when he wasn't being mean, it seemed to Catherine that Petie would only show up when she was busy digging around under the rose bushes or trying to send a piece of brick over a telephone wire without touching it. But when he came out back at last and called to her, she would break off whatever she was doing, just to listen to him talk. He replayed events outside the boundaries of their block like they were happening in front of them, his skinny muscles bulging through his tee shirt, spit whitening up the corners of his lips. The cats, though, had started to worry her, and one night before her mother came home, she had seen him out in the yard, hosing down the walk, and had gone outside and straight up to him at the fence.

"*Where would you get them?*" she demanded.

He knew, as he always seemed to, what she meant. "Oh, them're just alley cats, you get em in the alleys. Once I had to wrassle one away from a rat, and I almost got myself bit with rabies."

"Boy."

"Boy is right, sister. I gotta go now, later me'na boys is gonna play us some step ball and I got to run up Dolan's and get me some sodas and Chesterfields."

Catherine was mad at the way he'd talk to her just for a minute, and then let her know it was time for him to go do something more important. And, as always after talking to Petie, she moved through the rest of that afternoon from jubilant to deflated and back and forth between the two until she could make herself settle down.

Why doesn't he ever kiss me? she thought then, and even to her mind the question sounded a little stupid. She realized it was the first time she had wanted to kiss him, and she licked her mouth. Nothing, really, but then she thought maybe later she would feel something. She went inside, put on a pot of hot water to make the iced tea before her mother got home, finished up, went into the living room, and sat in one of the big red upholstered chairs by the window so she could see if he passed by. It would be after dinner before the step ball game started, but there would be dinner and dishes and small talk with her mother, and she could do all these things and think about Petie at the same time.

So Pretty

There was so much about boys generally she found so pretty then. They hung out in gangs, they got to go to the park and play real baseball at nine o'clock at night after the step ball games when the neighborhood melted into houses or down the street to the taverns or pizza parlors. Petie and his friends would walk off until she couldn't see them from the upstairs window, her head hanging out as far as she could. She badly wanted to go along and find out what they did down there at the end of the street after the sun went down. For all she knew, each one of them had a secret skill like braiding rope or swinging the life out of alley cats. Girls she knew had no such skill. She liked girls and had plenty of girlfriends in school, but few of them were free like the boys to be outrageous, or tell a boldfaced lie and not care, or let the spit pile up in their mouths. Girls stayed inside the yard, and if they moved their bodies it was mostly to the songs of the jump rope, getting them ready to k-i-s-s or count how many babies they were going to have or whose mother they were going to sock right in the nose if she didn't stay off their washer line. Catherine was never going to kiss anybody but Petie, she had never in her life seen a grown woman spend more time hanging up wash than she absolutely had to, and she had certainly never seen the unlikely spectacle of a couple of mothers battling it out over wet underwear.

But she loved the rhythm of jumping, and she could tell that Petie liked it, too. Sometimes he'd come out to his back yard to watch her and her friends take turns, and he'd just hang on the fence, swaying back and forth on the thin wire, looking like he wanted to say something.

Two days before she had been in the back yard with Sheila Fitzgerald and Mary Owens doing double-Dutch, and he had finally spoken up. They were turning the ropes and it was Catherine's turn to jump.

"Hey, Sister," he called out, loud, as she was counting twosies.

She stumbled and went down on one knee.

"Hey! Now look what you made me do!" she yelled back at him, spitting on the scraped skin.

"Crybaby. Lookit, you're doing it all wrong."

"Doing what all wrong?" Sheila said from her adenoids.

"The rope. You're not turning it fast enough."

"You can't turn it fast on this song, you jerk. You have to jump in time to the song."

"Well, that don't make me no difference. And that's a stupid song anyways. Here, lemme show you once."

Catherine hesitated. Nobody could come over when her mother was at work, unless it was Sheila and the other girls in the back yard. "You can't," she said.

He took in a breath. "You *cay-unt*!" he sneered. "Huh!" He spit and turned, and then turned back, and yelled like a little boy, "Bay-bee! "Baby, baby, bay-bee, can't come out and play-ee." He whistled once and then coughed and spit again. He knew it disgusted her when he did that.

"Forget it, Petie! You're *ignorant*!" she flung back at him.

As soon as the words jumped out of her mouth she knew she was dead. Sheila and Mary, a dough-faced girl who never said anything, screamed and flew out of the back gate. She tried to follow them, but he was over the fence and on her before she could get out. He grabbed her wrist and pulled her arm behind, forcing it up until she thought it would pop out.

"Take it back, Sister!" he screamed, but her arm hurt so much she couldn't say anything. "Take it back," he screamed again, just like a little kid.

She found herself down on the ground then, her face shoved into the cement and Petie yelling in her ear.

"Ok, ok!" she finally managed, but he still didn't get up. She felt his knee in her back and something about that felt not good, but all right, even though her arm felt like he'd broken it and she was terrified and furious. He yanked the arm once more and shoved the heel of his other hand into her head.

Then he got up. She rolled over to see his chest heaving, eyes lit up, exhilarated. "Now let me play," he said, almost casually.

Catherine crawled up and sat on the little garden curb, holding her right elbow in the other palm. Her knees were both scraped, she was busted up like a six-year-old, and she was crying like a little baby, too, but she couldn't stop. Sheila and Mary, who had watched the whole thing from the alley two houses up, came sidling back to the gate.

"Are you all right?" Sheila ventured, and Catherine nodded. They came back in the yard, looking to her like soft-boiled eggs, and picked up the rope. Petie laughed and then jumped in and began to count, but he missed after only a couple of steps. They stopped turning the rope.

"Do it again." They all looked at him but didn't move. "What? Lemme try it again, I can get it this time."

They picked up the rope even though Mary was holding back the tears so hard her nose was brick red, and Sheila looked like she wanted to do murder. He kept fumbling it for the next ten or fifteen minutes, the rope whacking him on the head or catching him up at the heels the way it used to do to the girls when they were all in first grade.

"No, wait a minute," he said again, and he laughed. And then they couldn't have said what it was: he looked so beautiful, so happy, and so oblivious that they all just about forgave him at the same time. Soon they were giggling, giving him pointers and howling as he substituted the dirtiest lyrics he could think of for the jumping songs: "On top of old Ma-a-ry, a-swingin' a chain..."

Mary's whole face went red at that and Sheila and Catherine just about threw up they were laughing so hard, and then Catherine became as full of love for him again as she had been furious. She touched her scraped face as if it were a secret. Her mother said that a man who would strike a woman was the lowest of the low, but Catherine didn't care. She could not have put words to it.

And just then one of Petie's pals came around the alley corner. For a moment she saw a glitter of something ugly in his eyes, and then he yanked the rope out of the girls' hands, still howling with laughter, turned, and flicked Catherine across one cheek with the end of the rope. He dropped it and flashed off, pretty as a paper bag on the wind.

She stood for just a moment, something coming up in her throat, emptied out again, it felt like, leaving the three girls there on that little strip of concrete with nothing. She managed to tell them she had to go inside, to wring out a load of clothes before her mother came home, she said. She ran in as they went out the back gate, hurled herself upstairs to her room, flung herself on the bed, and cried into the chenille spread until she fell asleep. When she woke up it was nearly dark, and she must have looked terrible because when she called her down for dinner her mother took one look and didn't interrogate her about falling asleep in the middle of the day, didn't ask about the scrapes on her cheek and forehead, didn't ask her to dry when she started the dishes, and didn't say no when she asked her if she could sit out on the front steps for a while before bed time. Petie didn't show up. When she went to bed Catherine shut the front windows tight and pulled the shades down to the sill.

Thursday Afternoon: She's Got to Have Something

She backed away a little bit from where they sat on either side of the fence, Petie on his steps, she facing him from the little curb underneath their screened-in back porch. She was not speaking to him because of how mean he had treated her, but last night she had dreamed about the cats and Petie, standing with his legs apart in one of the little doorways on Lemmon Street, a large congregation of colored men looking up at him, him whirling that cat around, and in the dream she had been worried, and was still worried. Did it belong to one of the men? Were they going to rush Petie? What would he do—oh, he could just jump over them and land on the roof across the street, that occurred to her as she dreamed. But if he fell, would they catch him? Would he scrape his face on broken glass? Would someone grind a cigarette out on his back? She woke up, sweating, shaking, and then cried as if he'd been next to her there in the bed and she'd lost him in the night. She hadn't gone back to sleep for a long time, but lay there, one hand on her chest, feeling her heart beat soften and listening for any sounds that might come through the wall from his house.

And when she woke again at six, she told herself that she loved him. She went through the day, to school, turned down an offer from Sheila to come over, sat in the living room for a little while and went out into the back yard while it was still sunny and a little bit warm. She was wearing her uniform blouse and skirt, with the sweater and her saddle shoes, and thinking to herself that soon Mr. Dolan's nephew, Paddy Dolan, was supposed to be in the big fight everybody was talking about, and how they were going to have company over and listen to it on the radio, because her mother knew some of Mr. Red's family and she'd want to talk about it with them though she would never go to a live prize fight herself. She said she didn't have the stomach for it.

Catherine had come out to the yard bored, so while she talked to herself she began doing sidewalk drawings with a piece of broken brick on the cement in between the back porch and the rose garden that filled up two-thirds of the narrow back yard. When Petie came out, she peered up at him from where she sat lower on the garden curb, but she didn't say anything else. It was chilly, and the light was starting to fade behind the houses. She looked at him again, and he spoke.

"Hey, kid. Not bad. What is it?" he asked, standing up and hanging over the thin fence wire. She didn't answer.

"Sister, c'mon. You mad?"

"Maybe," she said low.

"Wha-at?" he said with just enough laugh in his voice that she had to try not to giggle but wasn't insulting. "I didn't do nothin, I swear! I didn't hit ya that hard," he wheedled. "C'mon. Hey, I said I was sorry, you want a ingraved invitation or somethin?"

She couldn't hold out. "It's a tree." She sat back on her heels and squinted up at him. "You just keep piling "Vs" on top of each other and twist them around and there's all the branches."

"Huh. It looks like a tree, too. Git you a piece a green and put the leafs in." He grinned at her, slow and pretty, and she flushed.

Just then a crowd of boys came up to the back gate. They weren't his regular crowd, but a mostly dirty, slutty bunch of boys she had seen once or twice before, and that Paddy Dolan was one of them, and he seemed to be leading them up the alley.

"Hey, Petie, where's yer jump rope?" he called as he looked over and saw them. She was shocked. He was practically a grown man, and Petie was not much more than fifteen. Catherine stood up and took a step closer to Petie.

"Shut up, Paddy," he said with his usual bravado, but she could tell he was getting ready for a fight and that it was one he didn't seem to want to get into. She hadn't run into Paddy more than once or twice in her life, but her mother had said he wasn't much good, and had even told her to come right home if he was ever in his uncle's store.

Now Paddy leered over her back gate, and Petie leaned over the fence and gave her a push.

"Sister, go up on the porch." He'd dropped the hillbilly accent.

"But, Petie—"

"Catherine, go on, I said." He reached farther over across the fence and shoved her toward the steps, his eyes fixed on Paddy and the boys.

Paddy had his hand on the latch of her gate. "Pussy," he called low to her, his eyes on Petie. She thought she heard the boys with him gasp. And Petie was over his side of the fence in one jump. She thought he was going to give it to her, although she had said nothing to anyone about the alley cats and didn't understand how that Paddy could have known she knew about them. But Petie shoved her up the stairs and yanked open the screen door.

"Latch it and get inside," he said.

"C'mon, Petie, c'mon, don't," she pleaded.

"Just get in." He slammed the screen behind her.

By this time Paddy was up in the yard, looking down at her brick drawing, his head nearly level with Petie's as he stood at the foot of the steps. She latched the screen but didn't step back from the door.

"Now, ain't this cute?" Paddy bellowed. "Hey, lads, I think Petie here has turned into a pussy himself. Isn't that right, boyo?" His Irish accent was thick and he sounded a little drunk.

Petie stepped down then and walked right up to him, his chest not quite to Paddy's chest, staring right up into his face.

"C'mon."

Catherine was shocked that now Paddy was the one who looked like he didn't want what was coming next.

"What you mean?" he asked as if he really didn't know.

"C'mon," Petie repeated. "Carroll Park." Catherine heard in his voice that if they got to the park, one of them was going to get hurt but good.

"Petie, don't go!" she blurted out from the screen.

Paddy laughed. Apparently a reminder of her presence was enough to restore his swagger. "Why don't you come with us and show us that pussy of yours, girl?" he called up to her.

"I don't have one. Petie just told me about them —" she broke off as a couple of the boys started to howl, and a couple others turned red and stared down at the pavement. Her entire body burned as she realized what they meant.

"She don't have one! She don't have one! Well, she got to have somethin with those skinny legs and that flat chest for you to chase after her, Petie!" Paddy cried, and slapped his leg, but that was the last thing he said while he was in Catherine's yard.

Petie reached him in a step, slugged him across the face and knocked him back onto the walk, right on his elbows. He picked up a brick and jumped back up to the porch door as the gang rushed up to Paddy.

"Who's next?" Petie shouted, pumping the brick out over them like a preacher with a Bible.

No one answered. They pulled Paddy up and got him to the end of the yard and out the gate. Paddy pulled away from them in the alley and then slammed the open gate back into the frame. He waited for just a second, then screamed, "Marlon's the pussy! Marlon's the biggest fuckin pussy in the world!"

Then he sprinted away again down the alley to the boys, looking like one of them.

Thursday Afternoon: Hope Chest

Their shrieks and the clapping of their shoes seeming to mock Petie as he stood with one foot on her top step, the brick still in his hand. He looked in through the screen at her.

"You all right?"

"I'm all right." She didn't know what else to say.

He didn't move. She realized that he had never been this close to her back door before, and it seemed he was having the same thought. Suddenly he got a look, as if he were thinking of something new. He looked demented to her again then, his chest heaving the same way it had after he hurt her with the jump rope. She took a step back from the door.

"Let me in," he said, as if from far away. "C'mon." He sounded much older, his mountain-man accent back and more pronounced than ever, as if he were trying it out and seeing what it would do for him.

"Nuh-uh." She took another step back in.

"Don't make me break it down, Sister," he said, just as softly as before, and rattled the door.

Catherine's underpants were suddenly wet. The urine soaked through them and trickled down one leg into her white ankle sock, but she was able to stop it before she really wet herself enough for him to notice. She pushed the wet ankle behind the dry one, and though she was more frightened than she had been at any point until then, she was tempted to let him in. It was just the wet leg that stopped her from putting her hand out to the latch.

Petie leaned into the screen as if to push it out of the door frame. Then Catherine heard the key turn in the front door and the sound of her mother coming through the vestibule with grocery bags shuffling against her arms and stomach. "Hello! Catherine Lena!" she called.

Petie stopped and leaned a breath's worth back. He looked her full in the face. "If you tell I swear I'll come and beat the tar out of you. You hear me?"

As soon as he said it, the menace went out of his face and he seemed surprised. He looked around the porch and then at her as if wondering what the two of them were doing there.

"Huh," he said. "Well, see you later, Sister." He turned and walked out and down the steps.

"Petie, wait!" she cried after him.

He was gone, slamming the brick down onto the walk where it cracked on one corner into a little explosion of red chips and dust.

Catherine's leg and socks were damp and she could smell them, and she ran into the house and past her mother, mumbling something like she had to go first. She went up to the back bathroom and took off her underwear and socks, bare under her skirt. She didn't know what to do with the wet things. She couldn't rinse them out and she couldn't just throw them in the laundry or her mother would ask her what had happened. Without thinking, she got out a pair of scissors from the cupboard and started to cut them up, the yellow-brown smell of urine ripe on her hands. When she was done she held on to the damp clump of wet cotton for a minute. She turned to the window where the sun was already behind the back row of houses. There was a little breeze and pink tinges in the clouds.

She thought then of a hope chest, how you gathered linens and lingerie for your wedding to put in it. She didn't know what made her think of it. Then she opened the bathroom window and looked over to where Petie's back window met hers and where the porch roofs that slanted down in front of both windows were divided by nothing but a strip of old tar, sealing the joint between the shingles. She waited just another moment, then tossed the wad over on to his roof. Some of the pieces scattered but most landed together, round as a soft baseball. She watched them for a while, the edges fluttering a bit in the afternoon breeze.

After another while she became aware again of her bare skin below her skirt. It felt so strange to be standing by herself, happy about a pile of cut-up underwear unraveling on an asphalt roof, but in some way it didn't matter that she was the only one to know. And then all at once she felt as sad as she had ever let herself feel.

She closed the window, run a wet washcloth over her legs, put on some clean underclothes, and tripped back down the stairs to join her mother in the kitchen.

Friday Morning: Lies and Motor Oil

Waking the next morning, Catherine felt a fullness and emptiness that she couldn't put her finger on. She would have thought she would have been sad, even crying, but although she felt like crying, no tears would come, and she laughed out loud instead. All she knew was that it was a lucky chance that she only had a half day of school to get through.

She went down the hall to the bathroom and looked at herself in the mirror. Her two front teeth were a little crooked and a little off. She pressed the front of her pajama top over her chest. There wasn't much to make a silhouette of. She was sort of afraid to touch any place else, so she settled for staring at her face. There was a white line from the right corner of her mouth down to her chin from when she had drooled in the night. Her bangs were crooked, she hadn't noticed that before. Her eyebrows were too square and bushy. Her skin was nice, pale and roses in the cheeks.

She got out the same pair of scissors she had cut up her clothes with yesterday and started in on her bangs. She pressed them down and just cut off a sliver from the bottom, then fluffed them up to see if they were more even. She probably did this for about twenty minutes, until she heard her mother call from downstairs. She decided to make up a reason to go to the ten cent store, where she could buy a pair of tweezers and a tube of tangerine lipstick. She wasn't completely sure, she might get some face powder, too. She thought from the aromas coming up from the kitchen that her mother was making pancakes and sausage, and this meant she was aware of her suffering. She went over to the window, pulled up the shade, and peered sideways out over on to Petie's roof. There were a few strips of white cotton lying there still, with no breeze, so that they looked flat and dead. For a moment she came out of the trance she was in.

"Dear Jesus," she prayed, "please don't kill me before I have a chance to get to confession tomorrow."

Catherine sat down at her seat at the end of the kitchen table and looked blandly at the ring sausage cooling on the plate next to the stove, and without passion at the stack of pancakes with their perfect golden tops and thick white sides waiting for her to eat them.

"Good morning, honey," her mother said without turning around from the stove. "Are you feeling better? What, did you have a tummy ache yesterday?"

The irritation that shot through her felt comprehensive and original.

"Don't say tummy, Mother, please," she replied in her best Joan of Arc manner. She thought it was the right tone for the morning, but clearly she had miscued.

"*What* did you say, young lady?"

Her mother could pivot on the question *What?* faster than any grown person she ever met. It was one of the things she planned to emulate about her when she reached her age, but at the moment that spatula could come down just as easily on the back of Catherine's hand as on the next hotcake. She put her hands in her lap and said, "It's just that I'm getting too old to say 'tummy.' Ma'am."

"I'll let you know when you're too old for me to use the words God put in my head at any given moment, Miss, and that day will be when I'm in the cold, cold ground. Do I make myself clear?"

"Yes, ma'am." She didn't spit this out.

"What's gotten into you?"

Now she looked herself again, concerned, even shocked. Catherine felt better. Her mother scooped up three hotcakes and put them on her plate. They looked like cement. She started pouring on the thick brown King syrup. It looked like motor oil.

"Nothing." She thought she might cry, but then she'd just be set out in the back yard to sweep up or something equally disgusting. Besides, she needed to keep that yard unswept for as long as she could stand it. Her eyebrows felt like they weighed a pound apiece.

"Can I walk down to the ten cent store after school?" she blurted.

"What for?"

This was asked casually, as if the previous exchange was gone and forgotten, and she thought again how her mother never registered surprise or indignation at the times when she could have but she knew you hadn't quite said things the way you ought to have, and how she always let it go.

"Oh, nothing, I just want to look around."

"Well, sure. I'll be at work until about two o'clock, but if you find somebody to go with, you could before that."

"Oh! Well, Sheila asked if she could yesterday, so I could go with her."

She couldn't believe it. Not only had she lied to her mother but she had turned her back on God, whom she did not care to turn her back on. On the other hand, confession was tomorrow at 3:00 and she thought she could trust her luck until then. But, on the other hand, she was starting to feel dizzy. But, on the other hand, anything was better than sitting with this feeling.

And now Catherine had to figure out a way to convince Sheila they needed to go shopping two days before Palm Sunday.

Friday Afternoon: It Would Be a Kindness

But two hours after lunch they were strolling up Stricker towards Baltimore, the sun nearly hot on them and a few light clouds showing behind the tops of the houses. Sheila babbled in her muddy voice as usual, and Catherine thought there was too much light out to be making as much noise as she was. She felt like Edward G. Robinson. She thought she might even be starting to talk out of the side of her mouth. And Sheila was turning out to be the last human being she wanted to know, much less be walking down the street with.

"So *then* I says to her, you want to say that again? I says you want to come over here and say that to my *face*?" Sheila giggled. "It was just like Joan Crawford."

"If that's what one afternoon of being in the same yard with Petie Marlon did to you, you better watch it," Catherine said back. What was the matter with her? She wanted to hurt Sheila, just like that, but she didn't know why. Sheila hated Petie, she didn't even like when Catherine would talk to him when they were in the back yard. "Uh, uh, uh-uh," she'd say through closed lips.

"What?" Sheila said now, and stopped and stared at her. "What do you mean?" Her face was beet red and her lips had gone quivering at the corners. Catherine didn't think of the words she had just said, but that Sheila's talk was all like a movie poster or something. Who did she think she was?

"Who do you think you are, Sheila Fitzgerald, talking to me in that tone of voice?" She said that as mean and snotty as she could think of to say it, at the same time wondering whether and how she was losing her own mind. "You don't think Petie Marlon would look at you twice, do you, with that potato you have for a face and that garbage can you keep in your mouth—*do* you?"

Sheila stood there a minute and Catherine waited for her to hit her, or tell her off, or something, but she just turned around and ran back down the block. Catherine stared after her for just a minute, reveling in how deeply she hated her, and then turned on down Baltimore Street.

And then she felt like all the ladies that passed her could see what a terrible person she had become right there, and she didn't hate Sheila any more at all, she loved her and she wished she was walking with her. Any other day they would have been interested in all the things set out on the sidewalks in front of the stores and talked over all the old radios and new television sets in the window of the furniture store, coveting all the ladies' shoes in the window at Hess's. Now, alone, Catherine barely saw them. Still, she was hounded by this thing, this whatever it was that was making her do whatever it was she thought she had to do that was going to involve tweezers and tangerine lipstick.

When she entered Woolworth's, she was pleased as always at the smell of dry goods and soaps and hair dressings, and things felt right again for just a moment. She went over to the toy aisle at first, running her fingers over the dolls and trucks and story books. It wasn't too late to go home, to run up to Sheila's steps and knock on the door and tell her she was sorry, or crazy, or something.

She put her hand up to her eyes and felt her eyebrows. *Sheila's an idiot*, she thought. She bought the tweezers and the tube of lipstick. She bought some chewing gum for good measure, and a tiny little blue bottle of Evening in Paris. She wondered for a split second about seeing whether she could get away with buying a lady's pocketbook at the shoe store, but instead got a pink and white makeup bag, which she figured she could carry around like a clutch in the crook of her elbow. She explained to the lady behind the counter that these items were for her mother, who had asked her to pick them up while she was at work. The lady smiled at her and complimented her for being such a good girl and helping out. She smiled widely at the lady in her turn.

As soon as she was out of the store she stuffed the things into the makeup bag. Holding a handbag with makeup in it was such a novel experience that she thought she must look like a thief and that now any of the ladies passing her by would know her just for what she was. She slunk down Baltimore Street, close to the storefronts and walking fast with her head down. A little wiry stray dog followed her for a block or so, but it got interested in the dark green base of a street lamp after a while, and by the time she turned back down on to Stricker she was alone.

She had to pass Sheila's house on the way home—she lived in the block just across from Union Square—and she looked into her window as she passed. Sheila sat in a big chair in the window, looking tired, Catherine thought. Even though she wasn't looking out of the window, Catherine stuck out her tongue at her as far as she could stick it out. Then she heard rather than saw Sheila crying, and then she turned her head because she thought then she would start crying herself. But when she looked across the street to the square, she had the thought that she might go over there and just sashay around it a little while, because, of course, she was absolutely not allowed to do any such thing on her own when her mother was not at home. The sun was high in the sky and the day had turned extremely warm for April but with just the beginning of leaf buds on the trees and a cool wind. A few tulips had been planted near the cupola over the drinking fountain, and they were pretty. She thought she might just go over and look at them when she saw someone waving at her.

It was that Paddy Dolan, the one who had cursed at her and threatened Petie in her yard yesterday. He seemed to be holding up a dishrag in his hand or something like that, but he was definitely waving to her. Then he smiled, and for some reason she thought he had a nice smile, even from that far away. She waved back, and he called out something like, "Come on over." She was surprised, and then felt really weak in her legs somehow. She thought she must look like a mess, and turned her back to him, took the lipstick out, pulled off the lid, uncurled it, and applied what she hoped was a normal amount and shape of color that any woman or girl might put on her lips. She felt how heavy and waxy the lipstick was, and then she saw Sheila peeking out from the edge of the blind. She stuck her tongue out again, capped the lipstick and put it back in the bag as if she had been doing this out on the sidewalk every day of her life, and turned and walked across the street to the square.

Paddy Dolan seemingly hadn't taken his eyes off her, and he was still smiling. He looked quite dirty and disheveled, though, as she came up to him, and the belt of his pants was sitting unbuckled over his abdomen like a pair of open arms, and he smelled terrible. As Catherine stood in front of him where he sat on the bench, he didn't say anything to her.

"Hi," she said. Then she kicked the pavement with the toe of her saddle shoe like a little kid.

"Hi." He had a nice voice, though.

"I just saw you wave over there and thought you wanted to tell me something."

He didn't say anything for a moment. "You're that girlfriend of Marlon's, aren't you?"

Gosh, she thought. *Is that what everybody thinks? Maybe everybody thinks that.* "Um, yeah, I guess so."

"I shouldn't have talked to you like that before," he said. He pulled a packet of cigarettes out of his shirt pocket, held them out. "Care for one?"

"No, thanks, I'm not—" but she broke off before the word "allowed" escaped her mouth and ended with "smoking right now." That sounded pretty good.

"Well, perhaps you're wise," he said, and smiled at her again. For all of his dirty and disheveled clothes, she thought, *He's quite a good-looking boy. And that accent. I kind of like it.*

He was having trouble lighting his cigarette and she saw that he hadn't been holding a dishrag but that one was wrapped around his hand. "Here, let me," she said, and took the matches from him. He cupped his free hand over the cigarette, holding the end of it between his teeth. As she waved the match out, he drew in deeply and exhaled the smoke. They might have known each other forever, been related. She smiled at him.

"Do you live around here?" he asked. "I just wondered, because my uncle's store is around the block and I wondered if you ever go there."

Didn't he remember they had met in her back yard yesterday? She said, "Well, you know, I live next to Petie down on Stricker."

"Oh! Oh, yeh, that's right, lass. What was I thinking? We've met, haven't we? Well, it's a pleasure, I want you to know that. And I'll tell my uncle to look out for you at the store, give you special treatment."

Catherine was pleased in spite of herself. Then she thought, maybe Petie had been the jerk yesterday. He was so cruel to her—he was cruel, wasn't he? And he never came out again after all that to see if she was all right, even though she had stood out on the back porch after supper, way after the sun went down, with nothing else but to listen to Mr. Emerson on the other side of Petie's house yell at his tree and cry about how it didn't love him anymore.

"Oh, I'll—thank you," she said, "I'll be sure to ask my mother if I can go there more."

"I've never met your mother, I don't think," he said. "I'd like to meet her. You should meet my mother, too. Sometime. Maybe after the fight."

Catherine wasn't really following him, but it was a little late in the day and she figured maybe he'd been down at the tavern a while already. She opened her mouth to answer, but he started talking again.

"I remember when you had red hair, lass, back when you were just a slip of a thing." He looked up at her, frowning as if trying to remember something else. His lips were parted, slack in a way that made him look vulnerable and completely sincere. The hand holding the cigarette was shading his eyes as if the sun were in them, though he was facing away from the sun from where he sat. "It's too bad it went brown. Your hair, I mean."

She didn't want to correct him, somehow. The idea that she had had red hair once, even though it was in the mind of this stranger who had called her a pussy the day before, and even remembering that seemed like it had happened a long time ago to someone else, felt like something she didn't know how to say — *dashing*, she thought in a moment.

Yesterday, five minutes ago, Petie had occupied her whole thought, and now she felt him slipping past her like the people downtown on the crosswalk. No matter what they looked like to you, however arresting or attractive they seemed, you knew you'd never see them again, and the most you might do was to remember something about them for long enough to invent a story about them for a while as you lay in bed waiting for sleep to come. And now here was this man, whom she had never given a thought to before yesterday, making her feel not only more like a grown woman than she had ever felt with Petie or anyone, but attractive, interesting. He didn't shoo her away, he didn't tell her he had to get going. She held her mouth as still as she could and did not scratch her elbow.

"Don't kid yourself, Niamh. You're quite something, you know."

She had no idea what a neeve was, but suspected it might be some rare and special Irish word, like acushla. A piece of waxed paper that must have wrapped up some sliced meat or cheese at some point tussled past them on the walk.

"Don't you wish somebody would pick up the trash in this place?" she said. "I mean, it's not much trash on the sidewalks all the time, just, you know, gum and cigarettes, but it all seems to collect up in here somehows." After this spot of brilliance she wanted the sidewalk to open up and swallow her, but it seemed to impress Paddy, and he paused as if to give it the thought it deserved.

"Well, I don't know, lass," he said after a grave moment. "Who would you approach to see if it could be done?"

That hadn't occurred to her. Who was in charge of these kinds of things? "Maybe the librarian?" That was as close to a local public official as she could manage. "I don't think you'd ask the police, would you?"

"Nay, lass, that's very smart."

Her cheeks burned with pleasure and she wished she had gotten the face powder after all, or that there had been time over there in front of Sheila's to dab on some of the perfume. She wanted to push her eyebrows up but he hadn't taken his eyes off her and so she didn't dare.

He smiled at her again. "The librarian, now. If it wasn't she who was in charge, she could look it up for us to find out who was, now, couldn't she?"

That was very smart, she thought. Of course the librarian could look it up—that's what she did, wasn't it, when she wasn't looking for a book? And he said, "Us."

"Well, yes, she could," she said. "Um—well, I could run around there tomorrow and ask her about it. If you wanted. And then I could let you know."

"Would you?" His smiled broadened. "That would be a kindness, lass. I wish you would."

Catherine was pleased that she could be doing something for Paddy, and no more than it struck her that this was odd or strange did it seem wrong that they were just getting to know each other, two people who had met all of a sudden and liked each other, both willing to engage in a larger enterprise on the other's behalf simply because that's what people did, when they liked each other.

Paddy looked down at his stomach, seemed to notice the open belt for the first time. "Oh, will you look at me, lass? What a sight I am. I don't seem to be able to do nothing for myself today."

Catherine took a step back then, not because she was nervous or embarrassed, which she was, a little, but because she felt he might want some privacy. He got the hole-end of the belt into the buckle and pulled it to, but didn't put the middle piece of the buckle into one of the holes or push it into the loop. When he was done with this he looked up again, cupping his eyes as before.

"Do you go to Fourteen's, lass?"

"Um, yes, yes, sometimes we go. To the 9:00. Usually. I mean, because that's what my mother likes to go to. But I go to St. Martin's. Because I'm getting confirmed from school and that's, um, we go to church there when it's for school." Again, she thought he would laugh at her for such lunacy, but he seemed again to give what she said some thought, as if she had related serious news that took some thinking about.

"Oh! Confirmation," he said finally. "Well, that's nice, now, isn't it? My confirmation name is Patrick. Should have chosen something else, but then I didn't know I'd be coming over here, did I?"

Catherine guessed he meant something about the park, or, no, of course, he meant his family coming over here from Ireland. St. Patrick, that was right. But she had thought Paddy was slang or something for Patrick already.

"What name are you taking, Niamh?" That word again, she loved that word.

"Pauline," she said. "For St. Vincent de Paul, because I'm already Catherine, you know, from St. Catherine Labouré of the Miraculous Medal. And my father was part French." She had invented this last some years ago.

"From France, was he? There's a country, now, France. You didn't get your red hair from that side of the family, though." He winked at her, and his belt slid open a little bit. "Well. Maybe I'll see you in church then. And don't cut your hair, will you? You used to have such long, pretty hair."

She wondered how he could have known, but this, too, pleased her so much that she determined right then to grow it out and never to cut it again.

"Okay," she said. "Goodbye, Paddy. And I'll be sure to talk to the librarian about what you said."

He looked confused again for just a little bit. "Oh. Oh, sure, lass, would you do that? That would be a kindness."

A kindness, she thought. What a lovely way he had of putting things. It just showed, when men were with each other they acted different. How they were with women, that was how they really were. The sobriety of this thought pleased her again, and she said goodbye to him again, and then walked the rest of the way home pivoting on her toes as best as she could manage and turning the points of her saddle shoes, filled with new pleasure that coursed through every part of her. As she walked, she decided she would go to confession early tomorrow to be the first one in line, then hurry on over to the library to consult Miss D'Angelo about cleaning up the square. As she reached her door, Petie's mother was coming out in her cocoon of orange hair and lipstick.

"Hello, Mrs. Marlon!" she called out sunnily, as if to let anybody else who might be within earshot know that she had never been better. "Is Petie around?" she asked, pleased with her insouciance, feeling dashing.

Mrs. Marlon's eyebrows came together. "What's that you've got all over your mouth, young lady?"

The back of her hand shot up to her lips, though she didn't wipe it across. "Oh, gosh, I forgot I had that on!" She tried to giggle and look suitably concerned at the same time. "That was just because of confirmation practice." She frowned, and *Oh, my God*, she thought, *you idiot.*

"What's confirmation?" Mrs. Marlon asked. That was right, Catherine remembered, Petie's family was something else, some religion that didn't have sacraments or something.

"It's a play kind of thing," she invented then, relieved. "You have to wear it on the stage. I guess I just forgot to take it off a while."

"Oh! Well, you better wash it off before some boy sees you and gets the wrong idea. You don't want nobody getting the wrong idea, believe you me." She sighed as if at a memory then, and smiled at Catherine.

"Okay, I will," she smiled back. "Thank you, Mrs. Marlon."

"Bye-bye, now, hon."

Mrs. Marlon walked on up the block toward the streetcar stop, her slim hips swiveling magnificently under the full skirt of her dress and above her stylish heels, these scuffed a little and worn down on the outsides of the heels. There was no way Catherine could ever save enough money to buy a pair of shoes on her own, but if she did, she thought *I'd want a pair just like those*, but new, and polished, with a dress to match. The sun went behind a cloud, and then all the excitement and happiness she had felt coming down the block was gone. She went inside, ran upstairs to the bathroom, soaped up her mouth with water and the bar of Ivory that sat on the sink, rinsed off, licked her lips. The bitter taste was bad and good at the same time. She pulled out the scissors again, looked at them, put them back. She flushed the toilet just for instance, then went downstairs to the closet in the middle room, got out her mother's heavy scissors from her sewing basket, went out on the back steps, and proceeded to cut her jump rope up into exactly twenty-one pieces.

Friday Evening: Broken Hearts, Broken Hands

By the end of the day everyone had heard that Paddy wasn't going to fight, and that his dad had passed away in his sleep. Catherine was horrified to think that she believed Paddy had been drinking when she saw him at the square. She felt so deeply for him, she wanted to go to his house right away and make sure he was fine, but she didn't know where he lived, for one thing, and for another, when she mentioned it to her mother, she just answered, "Isn't that too bad?" in the tone of voice that meant no, it wasn't. Catherine knew better than to argue and finished wiping the dishes in silence.

Petie hadn't come home for lunch or for supper and his bed hadn't been slept in. She learned this listening in after his mother and father had rapped on their door and asked if they had seen him. Now they were out worrying on the front sidewalk just after supper, asking her mother and the Davisons from across the street what they thought they should do. She watched them on the walk, her mother peering up and down the street, Mrs. Marlon crying and streaking the rouge on her face. Mr. Marlon, whom Catherine hardly ever saw but always seemed pleasant and passive under his shock of oily black hair, looked angry, his cheeks nearly as red with anger as Mrs. Marlon's were with rouge.

After a minute or so, when she thought she heard somebody say they should bring in the police, two boys she thought she recognized walked up, the one tall and blonde, the other dark and slender but with oddly soft and plump hands and facial features. This boy addressed himself to Mrs. Davison, who gave him a slap across the back of his head, whereat Mr. Davison grabbed her arm and put her a little behind him. Catherine pushed the window up as slowly as she could to hear them better.

"Don't do that, Agnes," Mr. Davison was saying. "Okay, Ronnie, he's at Sonny's"—Sonny, she knew, was the Davison's oldest boy, who had graduated from Poly Tech and had a job doing something that paid pretty good—"and you say he's all right? Did the doctor come take a look at eem?"

"Yes, sir, Dr. Agnew came and he saw he had a couple of broke ribs, and he taped them up for him, and he said don't move him for a couple two-three days. And he can't eat nothing much until Monday, so we're giving him sodas and subs and all," Ronnie said.

"Subs! You boys don't have the sense God gave a goat, I swear to God! I'm going down there right this minute," Mrs. Marlon burst out, "and if I get my hands on that Paddy Dolan I'll tear him limb from limb."

"Now, Sally, they don't know the whole story—" Mr. Marlon began.

"Whole story my hind leg!" she spat. "That boy is no good and I don't care who he is or what he thinks he can get away with. I'm calling the patrol car. I'm going to try out a warrant against him—" and here she broke down, standing there in the sidewalk, Mr. Marlon patting her arm weakly, the color gone from his face. It was getting dark, the barber shop on the corner closing up and putting the lights out, and cars had begun to roll by on their way to Saturday night pleasures.

Catherine's mother said something to Mr. Marlon she couldn't hear and put both hands on Mrs. Marlon's arms, which she had never seen her do to anyone in public. She didn't even shake her a little, she just held on to her and spoke softly. "Now, Sally. Come on. It was just a fight and he's all right. We'll walk down there together. Come on."

As Mrs. Marlon calmed down, her mother handed Mrs. Marlon a handkerchief from her apron pocket and waited while she dried her eyes. "Catherine, get my bag and come on," she said without looking over.

Catherine jumped, got the purse and a sweater for herself, grabbed a head scarf, too, and joined them out on the walk. The two boys, Ronnie and the other one who hadn't spoken, looked at her curiously and it seemed with some sympathy, and all, the Marlons, the Davisons, the boys, and her mother and Catherine, started down the block.

As they walked, she stayed in back. After a moment the tall one fell in beside her.

"I'm real sorry about that there yesterday. I mean, in your yard."

She couldn't remember him being there, so didn't answer.

"I mean, none of us had any ideers Paddy would go for you like that. I never heard a man talk to a girl that way before. He must've had a few or I don't know what." He paused. "I should've come into the yard and took him out."

Catherine was thinking about Paddy, how sweet he had looked on the park bench. She said, "I don't think he meant it. I saw him today anyways, and he apologized and all."

"He sure knocked the tar out of Petie," the boy said.

This made her a little glad. "His daddy died, you know. Paddy's. He died this morning, I heard."

He straightened and looked down the street. "God bless him," he said. "I'm nobody to speak ill of the dead." He put his hands up to his shirt pocket. "I need a cigarette," he said.

She didn't reply, and after a moment he moved back into step with the boy Ronnie. She thought of Paddy, how he'd been so disheveled and unkempt this morning, how he called her "neeve" and thought she'd had long, red hair. And now here he was, not going to be able to fight Red Fitz, and his hand hurt, and his daddy died. She started to cry quietly, wiping the tears from her face. Her mother turned and saw her, and let go Mrs. Marlon's elbow and came back to her.

"Don't worry, sweetheart," she said, "Petie's going to be okay, you'll see. A couple of days and he'll be back to his old self. And maybe we'll all go to the park for a picnic soon or something. Okay?"

"Okay," Catherine said. Her mother gave her a little hug as they reached the door of Sonny Davison's house, and she did her best not to shrug off her arm. She didn't give a care about Petie Marlon.

The front room where she had been parked and told to sit still while the boys and adults went upstairs to see Petie was much nicer than she would have thought. There was a sofa, and a low radio console between the two front windows, and there was a nice-looking chair on either side of the radio, each one uphol-stered in a flat kind of fabric that was colored a deep burgundy, and the sofa in a red cloth to match. The side tables and the cof-fee table were old, the finish deep and almost black, with a sheen of red and trimmed in a kind of curvy lattice-work that made her head hurt to look at after a while. There was a metal ashtray stand by the doorway, holding an amber glass filled with ciga-rette stubs, none with the imprint of a woman's lipstick. Unlike her house, the mantel, rather than being above an ornamental furnace grate, was set over an open space that must have been a fireplace at one time but now looked like it housed some kind of gas contraption. A picture that many people had then, of a pair of old hands, thin and folded in prayer, was on the wall above the mantel. She looked down at her hands, long and thin but the nails ragged where she bit them. She looked out the window.

A few people walked up and down the street, talking, smok-ing. Lights went on in front rooms on first and second floors as the last of the sunlight slid up the house fronts. An old black car pulled up in front of one of them, and a man in a light overcoat and brown hat got out, whistling between his teeth, shut the door, shoved a thick newspaper under his arm, went up a set of steps, let himself in the house. A dog barked over and over, far enough away that the sound became part of the evening, only intruding every now and again, mostly when the boy whose name she still had not heard anybody mention would put his head in the doorway to ask she if she wanted a soda or a piece of candy or anything.

"No," she said this time. She felt she had said "thank you" plenty enough already. "How long are they going to take?" But this sounded petty even to her. "Do you think, or don't you know?" she amended.

"I think somebody said call the doctor again. But I don't think anybody has went up to the call box yet." He looked around the room once, maybe to see if everything was still in place from the last time he was here. "You sure you don't want nothing? I think it's some ice tea in the icebox."

"Okay, I'll take some ice tea."

His eyebrows went up. It seemed he could tell the difference between rude and polite after all.

"You like sugar in it?"

"Yes, please. Thank you very much." Her face was burning.

At this he grinned at her, said, "Well, what do you know?" and went back out the door before she could think of a comeback.

She put him at seventeen or eighteen, though she thought the other boy, Ronnie, might have been closer to Petie's age. She would have tried to guess if she had really been paying attention to anything but the setting of the sun and realizing she would never be able to get to the square tonight. The grief of Paddy's loss was sitting so heavily in her that she thought for a moment it was her own father who had died, though of course her own father had died, and she had never grieved him because she had never known him. Her mother always told her he had been a "good" man, but she didn't really talk about him that much and Catherine had never given him a whole lot of thought. Now she felt exquisitely what it must be like to lose someone you had actually known. She thought Paddy's father must have been a wonderful person. She bet he'd had a very fine job somewhere, maybe in a store on Baltimore Street or downtown, or maybe he even worked on the B & O Railroad, where some of the fathers she knew worked. She knew he'd never do anything low like tend bar in a tavern or—well, she didn't know what was worse than that, unless it was not having a job at all, like Mr. Emerson, but he was a drunk and quite a few fathers drank. Not Mr. Dolan, though, she bet, forgetting she had seen him at least a half dozen times in Dolan's store. She bet he had had a lovely head of hair, just like Paddy, and she thought he must have wise, kind eyes, and a straight nose, and smooth skin. She bet he was tall, and strong. She wondered how Paddy would ever get over losing him.

By the time the boy came back with the iced tea she was wiping tears off her face with the palms of her hands. There wasn't a lamp lit, though, so that the room was softened only by the light of the street lamp just outside, and she didn't think he noticed. He didn't say anything about it.

"Here you go," he said in the voice of a waiter in a diner. "Let me know if it's enough sugar for you."

Catherine sipped at it half-heartedly, but then was surprised at how good it tasted. There was a nice soft layer of sugar in the bottom of the glass, too, and she found herself looking forward to the way she knew it would slide into her mouth in a moment.

"It's real good. Thanks," she said.

At this he smiled, and she saw that he had a really lovely smile. "I'm Paul," he said.

"I'm Catherine."

"I know. I mean, I heard your mother say." He paused, looked out the window over her head. "I need a cigarette," he said.

"Oh, go head," she said. "Don't mind me. I'm not smoking at the moment, but I don't mind it." She took another drink of the tea. It was very good. When she reached the sugar, just as he lit the end of his cigarette, she didn't think anything had ever tasted so good. "Can I have another glass?"

He looked surprised but pleased. "Sure thing. Let me just — no, you know, sure. You want a fresh glass?"

"Oh! Oh, no, this one is okay. But you could rinse it out if you wanted."

"Oh! Yeah, sure, I will. And you like sugar, right?"

"Yes, that was just right, how much you put in. Thank you."

And she smiled at him, and he smiled at her, and she thought how wonderful it was, when you loved someone the way she loved Paddy, how suddenly everyone was nice to you, and kind, and as if they liked nothing better than to make sure that you were happy. She folded her arms to her chest, took in a deep, pleased breath, and felt it, that deep happiness.

The next person to come to the door of Sonny's living room was not Paul, but Catherine's mother. "Come on, honey. I've got to go home so I can check in on Mrs. Dolan in a bit. God knows she's got nobody to look after her now. But we should call the doctor and get out of everyone's way a while. Mrs. Marlon said she'd let us know what he says when they get back home."

Catherine agreed happily, got up and passed Paul in the doorway, noticed he held a glass of iced tea, smiled at him. "It was nice to meet you," she said.

He didn't reply. He began to drink the tea as she turned her back on him and followed her mother out the door.

"That's a nice boy," she said as they reached the sidewalk.

"Who?"

"That boy who was looking after you."

"*What*?" Nobody had been looking after her, she had been sitting alone in someone's front room. Couldn't she even sit alone in someone's front room without her making a federal case out of it? "For your information, Mother, I was just sitting there. He came in a couple of times and talked to me, and I talked back to him to be polite. That Is All."

"Watch your mouth, Miss," was all she said. Catherine could tell she'd wanted to talk everything over as they left the house but was glad she didn't pursue it now, even though it was because she was angry. They walked together not talking, and Catherine was suddenly enraged by how slowly they walked. She started to walk faster, so that in a few steps she was about three or so paces ahead, swinging her arms at her sides and swiveling as she had done on the way home from the square that afternoon, wishing that she too had a pocketbook to maneuver or keep track of at her side.

"Where's the fire?" her mother finally asked, and she couldn't tell if she was just laughing or laughing at her. "Come here, walk next to me like you have the manners God gave a goat."

"Wha-at?" Catherine thoroughly wanted to do something rude right then if she could have gotten away with it. "Oh, was I walking too fast? I'm sorry."

"Mm-hmm. Let me just stop at the call box here."

That did it.

"Mother! We have a *phone*. Why don't we just walk two blocks and use our *own phone*?"

Her mother grabbed Catherine's nearest arm, tight, looked straight in her face. "I don't know what's gotten into you and I don't want to know. But you save that kind of language for someone who's going to put up with it if you know what's good for you. The next time you open your mouth to me like that, believe you me, little girl, it'll be your last."

"Mommy—we're out on the street!" They were just a half a block from Paddy's uncle's store—what if he was there, what if he saw Catherine being shaken by the arm like a little baby this way? Well, she would die, that's what.

"Yes, we are," she said. "And you remember that next time if you know what's good for you."

She let go, went into the call box, dialed a number. Catherine couldn't even listen to her. She just wanted to die.

She looked up the street and could make out the heavy green door of Dolan's store. There didn't appear to be any light in it, or in the two windows above it on the second floor. A couple of pigeons rested on the top ledge of the brickfront. She wondered if Paddy ever went up on that roof and looked down at the street below. Her house had three stories, and sometimes she went up into the empty bedroom her mother used for storage, where she used to play house and dress-up when she was a little girl, and where she looked out the windows now when she wanted to think or just to get some distance between herself and the rest of the world. The second floor wasn't high up enough for her for that, and she bet it wasn't high up enough for Paddy, either. He wasn't there, though, and it was no good trying to make out that he was. She was getting chilly as she stood next to the call box, half-listening to her mother on the phone with Dr. Agnew, whose doughy hands and the blush that always rose to his fat cheeks whenever he had to put a stethoscope next to her chest she hated, and she shuddered and stamped her feet on the pavement.

She reached in and tugged at her mother's elbow. Her mother turned around, her eyebrows high.

"I'm going home," Catherine mouthed.

Her mother nodded briefly and waved her free hand. "No, sir, I don't think he's taken a fever," she said into the mouthpiece as Catherine turned away.

She looked up and down Pratt Street. To the east the street lowered in the soft light, the street lamps not yet on just there but further out towards downtown they were turning on. Church spires rose up above the rows of houses here and there, a few clouds thick as heavy snow hung low in the sky, bursts of grey and blue and threads of rose light around them. A beat policeman walked away about two blocks down and the sight of him made her angry and nervous. The wet air clung to her, seemed to pull on her skin. She held her elbows tight to her sides and crossed the street.

The twilight had turned to darkness. The funeral parlor at the end of the block stood in elegant silence as she passed. Her father had been laid out there, and so, she supposed now for the first time, Paddy's father would be taken there, too, might even be there now. She stopped for half a second, shuddered, then walked on, past Smith's, past Mr. Emerson's, past Miss Julie's, past Petie's. A television set glowed blue and white out of Petie's window, a light that whenever she had seen it before this night had often brought her nearly to the point of swooning, and she wondered again where Paddy's house was. When she reached her steps she hurried up them without pausing, turned the doorknob, closed the front door behind her and then the vestibule door to the living room after that, picked up the skeleton key from the end table where her mother always kept it, put the key inside her skirt pocket, and walked the length of the house and out through the back door, down the yard and out the gate.

Friday Night: Babes in Arms

As many times as she had looked at this alley, stared at it, gazed through it, and made up stories about what happened in it, she had never been out in it this far before. Everything looked strange, too close and very small. She raced up the few steps to Lemmon Street, not even half a block away from her gate, and when she got there she was so nervous she thought she might fall down and she reached out to hold on to the fence.

Only the lamplight from one street light illuminated the narrow alley, and she was so cold. She looked back down her alley.

She had never seen the back of our house from any distance, and she was ashamed of how shabby it looked. She thought about this, didn't know why. The back porch looked tired of holding itself up. It wasn't finished in brick like the rest of the house, but in wooden slats, peeling tan paint. The bricks above it and down the side of the house as far as she could see were darker than the bright red ones in the front that she never ceased to be pleased with. These here looked cheap and old. She couldn't see anything of her cut-up underpants on Petie's porch roof. It was too dark to see.

Someone belched nearby, but the sound echoed and she couldn't tell right away from where it had come. She looked down and saw Mr. Emerson sitting on his back steps, nodding off into the railing. The glass he held glinted in the light. It looked as if it might fall at any moment, and she was tempted to wait to see if it would, but instead she turned and walked quickly without running up Lemmon, peered around the corner to see if her mother was still down the block at the call box. No one was in the street. She headed to the square, staying close to the fences and buildings. She crossed Lombard kitty-corner, stopped, and stood on the threshold of the square for a moment, then walked in.

He was sitting on the same bench, dressed the same, so that she wondered whether he hadn't been there all day. Then she thought maybe he'd gone and come back because she might be there, and this pleased her so much she lost all nervousness and flushed warm all over, and smiled, and walked up to him.

"Hello," she said.

He didn't appear startled, but again as he had that afternoon seemed to have trouble placing her. He put his hand up above his eyes again as well, as if he were shielding them from the sun.

"Is it you, Niamh?"

"Yes, it's me." So he did know her after all.

"Couldn't sleep either, lass?"

"Um." Perhaps it was later than she thought it was, or maybe Paddy got up and went to bed early. Just like that, she could picture him sitting in the soft light of a back window before dawn, in his undershirt, his elbow on the table and a plate of eggs and a cup of tea or coffee before him. "No, no, I couldn't. How are you feeling, Paddy?"

"It hurts, lass. I don't think nothing has every hurt me so bad."

Catherine didn't know quite what to say to that. She felt honorable, and stood taller.

"Have you ever felt anything like this, lass?"

She considered. She thought of Petie pushing her into the concrete, and of the look on his face staring at her through the back screen, and she thought those might be as bad as losing your father, but she just didn't know. "I don't think so," she said.

"I should probably call the doctor, eh? Get it seen to?"

He sat somewhat in the shadows and she had forgotten about his wounded hand. She adjusted her thoughts, temporized.

"Dr. Agnew is not at home," she said.

"Isn't he, now? How do you know? No sickness in your home, lass, I hope?" He looked genuinely worried and she was pleased again.

"No, no. It's just that Petie Marlon isn't well, and—"

He broke in, silent laughter seemed to ripple through him. "Not well. No, I'll go to bail he's not well, the son-of-a-bitch pussy."

All of the soft warmth of his Irish cadence was gone. He didn't sound any different from any other boy she had ever heard use that kind of talk. But he looked up again, and smiled, and she could feel him blush.

"Eh, lass, I'm sorry about that. Sometimes I just don't know when to watch my own mouth."

That she could forgive.

"So Marlon's with the doctor? Well, perhaps he's wise, then. Have you seen him?"

"No, they made me wait downstairs. I didn't care, anyway," she said, and in case the words sounded defiant, added, "I mean, I didn't care to go see him."

"Well, no, Niamh, it's no place for the likes of you, a sick room." He put his hand down finally, seemed to indicate a spot on the bench where she could sit.

"Please," he said.

She sat down next to him, the cold seat damp against her bottom and thighs. She realized that, apart from nights down the shore when she and her cousins got to sit up late listening to her mother's relatives talk into the night, looking out over the glistening bay water and falling asleep to the cadences of low speech and thick rhythm of the night bugs, she had never been outside her own yard or off her own front steps this long after dark. She looked around over the square, which was empty except for, she saw, a couple sitting across the park, very close together. They looked small, but they were clear in the lamplight. They had been quiet up until now, but the woman laughed, and then she did, too. She looked over to Paddy, who smiled back at her.

"Just an old couple out of an evening, you and me, aren't we?" he said, and nodded over at the other couple as if he had been watching her watch them.

"Sure," she stammered. He seemed to know her thoughts, she couldn't believe it, how quickly they had grown so close. She was almost unendurably happy. She looked back over at the couple, who were now tightly embraced, the woman seeming to be pushing her hands hard against the man's chest, but Catherine couldn't tell if it was to get away. She glanced at Paddy, who was watching them, smiling. She looked at him and felt a tenderness she believed she had never felt before. *I love you, Paddy Dolan*, she thought, and this thought seemed as natural and timely as any had been.

The side of his face was shadowed away from the lamplight. He didn't say anything more, but she was content just to be there with him, sometimes looking down at her lap, then back at the side of his face. They sat for maybe five minutes, and then his eyes seemed to grow intent, and he smiled, but it wasn't a pleasant smile, and she didn't know what changed or what the smile had to do with her.

"Eh, now, there they go," he said. "That Carmen is a one, she is, look at her," he said, and she looked in the direction he was looking, back toward the other couple.

The woman was now sitting on the man's lap, her back to them. She was moving her torso up and down, it seemed as if she were on a carnival pony, going slowly but every movement regular and the exact same space of distance. They seemed to be talking to each other, but she couldn't make out the words. Her voice was high-pitched, his low, both sounding urgent or impatient. Then his hands were underneath her skirt, and he was helping to lift her up. His grip seemed to grow tighter, and the next time she moved up she saw the length of his arms against her legs, that her stockings had come off the clips of her garter, which Catherine couldn't see, and then she saw the woman's buttocks, white as paper, as the man lifted her skirt up over them and let one of his hands pass between them, and then the patch of darkness between his legs and the glint of his discarded belt buckle as her bottom lifted away from him.

"That's the stuff, lad," Paddy said then.

Catherine whipped her head away from the sight of them to Paddy, the smile on his face intent now, his head nodding almost violently. She wanted to say something, but didn't know what.

"Paddy— " she began.

"Can't you help your old man out, lad?" he said between his teeth.

"What's the matter, Paddy? Are you sick?" she asked. She was cold again all at once, through and through, and she didn't want to help with anything Paddy at all. Then everything seemed to go very still and slow. She could hear the woman those few yards away, she seemed to be crying and then cried out, but Catherine couldn't make herself look back over there to see if the woman was all right, so she kept looking at Paddy.

"I said, help me out, lad," he spat out without turning his head to her, and then he reached over for her hand, pulling it over his waist.

"Wait a minute, Paddy, wait a minute, don't," she began and then her hand touched something hot and Paddy was molding her fingers around it. She nearly faced him, and felt the thing, like the calf of an infant you might take hold of and shake to make the baby laugh, the skin soft and the inside firm but something about it delicate so that you didn't want to feel too hard for the bones, and as her hand was lifted up and along the length of it, she felt the end, like a bump, and she knew and didn't know what she was holding, and then some slick business that felt like what came out of her at the end of every month before she began bleeding covered her fingers, and she yelled out *No!* as Paddy moved and cried out just as the woman had done. She wrenched free, her left hand coming down hard against Paddy's injured one, and he screamed then, and she pushed up to her feet and turned around to run.

The other man was watching her, the woman limp against his chest the way a baby sleeps on the shoulder of its mother, and the man smiled at her as if they were in on the same secret. His slick black hair was parted in the middle, the thick black frames of his eyeglasses, the pock marks on his cheeks and nose emerged as clearly as if they were standing next to each other. He pulled one of his hands out from underneath the woman's skirt, calmly, and waved at her as she turned and ran out of the park and into the street.

It took all of two minutes to reach her front door, which she found standing open. As she reached for the doorknob, she felt her hand wet, and looked down at it, sticky and a thin thread of some white stuff clung to it. As she went in, she could hear the radio playing in the kitchen. She ran up the stairs to the bathroom, washed her hands, sat on the open toilet seat, stared at the wicker laundry hamper. She stayed there a long time.

Palm Sunday, April 6th

Preface, Palm Sunday evening: Introibo ad altare Dei

The assistant pastor stood in the darkness on the top step of Fourteen Holy Martyrs Church, having locked the door, praying the Suscipe silently as he ran through his plans for tomorrow's funeral, going over the words for the eulogy for a man he barely knew. That happened often enough and he wasn't worried about it. He lit a cigarette, kicked aside a strand of palm leaf, cursed himself for it. He begged forgiveness silently, picked the frond up and began to wind it around the fingers of his left hand, keeping the cigarette coal away from the leaf. He could pray while doing and thinking nearly anything else. He didn't move but to raise the cigarette to his mouth or look down the long blocks of Lombard to downtown, surprised he never noticed before how far you could see. A streetcar went by, empty but for the conductor. He felt at once that he knew what it would be like to be a street car. He wondered what street cars made of their singular paths when they were empty. He wondered about each and every living thing that occupied those houses, realized he felt no particular love for the people, but that he loved these houses and this street near to idolatry.

A taxi pulled up, and slowed, and a small, dark-haired woman got out of it, weaving on her feet a little bit, and a man followed, and the priest saw it was Paddy Dolan, the son of the man at whose funeral he'd be presiding tomorrow. Paddy swung the cab door shut and smacked the woman on her bottom as she shrieked and laughed, and then he looked up the block, saw the priest and caught his eye, and stood straighter, pushing the woman away from him a little. He said something to her, and she pointed, down the block and over to Union Square. He shook his head, shoving his one bandaged hand deep into his trouser pocket, and turned and began walking toward the church.

"Evening, Father," Paddy said as he hurried past.

"Good evening," he replied, and then looked down to where the woman still stood, and then he saw her take a step, lurch, re-gain her balance, but then seemingly unable to move again.

He went down the stairs and walked over to her, smiled again, said, "Can I help you with anything?"

She eyed him for just a moment, and even before she opened her mouth he could smell the liquor and other odors he didn't know on her breath.

"Why, hello, baby," she said. "What do you want to do? You want to go somewhere? I want to go into the square. You want to go?" She smiled at him in return, a lovely smile, but something in him felt cold at the sight of it.

Still, he could see she was in no fair case to get anywhere on her own, and he couldn't bring her inside the rectory. He thought he'd walk her that far, just down the block to the square, and find out where she lived, and get her home. It was a fine night for a little walk, anyway.

I. Deus, Deus meus, réspice in me: quare me dereliquísti? longe a salúte mea verba delictórum meórum

Sometime after midnight Catherine decided she was going to call herself Constance from now on. She had decided that Pauline was the stupidest name a person could possibly select as a confirmation name, and that Catherine was likely as useless as Pauline was stupid. She couldn't do anything about Catherine, of course, but she could be C. L. Something Bernstein for the rest of her life, however long that would be. Her mother had seen her for a moment, asked an innocuous question, and Catherine's reply had brought her mother's hand across her mouth.

"I never thought I would have to put a hand to you," was all she said.

She had deserved being hit, one day before Palm Sunday. Yes, a slap must be the least she deserved. She doubled over, her head pressing into the floor, and sobbed until her mother came back in, put her arms around her, cradled her, said, "I'm sorry, I'm sorry, I'm sorry," until she had not be able to stand it for another minute, and she broke away and ran up the stairs, not to her room, but to the front room of the third floor, where she pushed past all the boxes and old furniture to the chair she kept by the window, moved it to face north, and stared out into the emptying street toward Union Square.

The name Constance had come to her in what she would not until later in life know to call the night watches, as the first pains from her period began, and in the eleven months since she had begun menstruating, other than the first time, which had hit her at about four o'clock in the afternoon one day as she was taking a streetcar home from the library, she had never been awake but always had woken up first thing in the morning from pains that seemed to cut into her and crush her all at once, and she would get through the next twenty-four hours or so taking aspirins and holding on to hot water bottles that did nothing to stop or stem the pains, searching for a position on the bed that she could never find. *Constantly,* she thought, her whole life until she would be a very old woman, her months would be constantly marked with this pain, she saw that now, just like what they said, a woman's life was made of pain, and she had never believed that before. It had seemed stupid to her then, ignorant, uninformed, pessimistic.

And then she thought all at once, *Constance, that's what I'll take for my confirmation name.* A confirmation was what you had to carry with you, it was a vow forever, and you could never break a vow no matter how much you might want to. She had felt one thing, then another, and then another yesterday and none of them coming from any place within her that she had not even known she could trust, much less needed to trust, but now, feeling as if the center part of herself had somehow evaporated into untrustworthiness and that she knew nothing in the world for certain at all.

But then she thought, maybe having all those feelings at one time, like too much excitement at a birthday or a pajama party, that's all it had been. Sure. She had gotten herself over-excited, she thought now like a nurse. And then she had lost her mind a minute, and, well, she just should have known better. But how she had lost it, that was the other question that immediately presented itself, and it frightened her as she sat in the cold window, and the reassurances she invented were lost.

In the hours she sat there in the window she held her right hand out in front of her, until it went to sleep and she had to shake it to wake it up. The sensation of circulation returning was not painful but curious. The whole thing was curious. She could not get out of her head the sight of that man's hand slipping between the woman's legs and how dark it all was, and how slow it had seemed to happen and yet how much like a dream or a moving picture it had looked. She had always had this idea in the back of her mind, perhaps from the way her mother always spoke about her father with a certain warmth combined with disinterested factuality, that what happened between men and women wasn't all that much to talk about, but then there was Petie and he was thrilling and that was a fact, but still she hadn't had the slightest idea before tonight that the thrill of him had anything to do with what had gone on in the park. She felt sick.

Paddy Dolan, now, what had it been about him sitting there all dirty and bloody on that green bench that had seemed remarkable to her, that had seemed *dashing*? What a stupid word that was. *He's just a dirty old man*, and she was surprised that thinking this didn't hurt her feelings more than it did. Her hand burned, though, and this upset her, though she felt cut off from that feeling, too.

And Sheila, she thought then, *O Mary Mother of God*, she thought, *how in the Lord am I going to make it up to Sheila?*

"Who cares?" she said out loud. "Sheila's an idiot."

No, that was a very big lie. No, it wasn't.

Oh, my goodness.

And then she thought of Petie, next door to her there in the room, but then she realized she wasn't in her room, and she wasn't lying next to him with the wall just between them, that she wasn't even facing Petie's house, and that he wasn't even there in the house had she been in her room, and, finally, that she didn't even really know for sure that the room next to hers was his room because she had never even been inside his house as far as his living room.

She began to cry at this overwhelmingly melancholy thought, and lifted her eyes to the back windows of the houses that faced Lombard Street, just above the automobile garage on the corner of Lemmon. The skinny trees there were bare of leaves, but there was something very pretty about how they stood in the yards, at the back of the houses. There was a single light on in one of the second floor windows, which from where she was, slightly down the hill, was just about parallel to her, and she saw someone, whether man or woman she couldn't make out, sitting at a table in the window, one hand on the brow, the elbow leaning into the table, the other hand seemingly across and bent over. The person sat up straight then, picked up something, a newspaper or a sheaf of some other papers, and began to read.

She stopped crying as quickly as she had begun, and wiped her hand over the tears on her face, sniffed once, and then smiled, really happy. And a pain came just then, sharp and biting, not yet followed by the nausea and crushing feeling, so different from what she was used to being wakened by that she wondered if this month would be different, if the pain and cramping would last longer or shorter or who knew what. Something about this thought made her feel even more cheerful all at once, and she smiled again at the person reading in the window, and stayed there another while longer, feeling the quiet and the dark and the magnificence of two people awake sharing the same sleeping world.

She pivoted in the chair, crept out of the room in bare feet, down the stairs, to the landing of her mother's room where she could hear her snoring in that persistent but polite way she had, and then, as her footstep made a slight creak on the step, heard the snoring stop, and that stopped her, too, for a chilly and nearly unbearably present and awake and alive moment, her hand out on the wall pressing into it, and then her mother called out softly, "Catherine?" She tiptoed off the stair and back to her own bed, which she got into, placing her head lightly onto the pillow. She was not bleeding yet but her legs were hot and her head was cold and damp. She slid her knees down into the cold of the sheets, and placed both of her hands over her hot abdomen, pressing them in.

II. Dómine, ne longe fácias auxílium tuum a me

Catherine rolled over in the bed, pulling the sheets around her. She had spent all day yesterday, practically, in bed, the cramps had never hurt that badly before, and she wondered whether it was because she had done such a wrong thing, had felt such wrong things, had let such wrong things happen to her, and it was all her own self to blame and nobody else's. A reason for that kind of pain, that's what she was looking for. The flesh between her legs still felt hot, heavy, and large. She thought she might be starting a fever —*from being outside after dark in April, you stupid thing*—and started to cry. It was Palm Sunday and she had to get up for church. She could tell the way the sun slanted on Mrs. Lingle's wall across the side yard it must be nearly or even past time to get ready. The lower half of her body, from her stomach to her knees, was burning, but when she put a hand to her head it was cool, even cold, sweaty. She pushed herself up and swung her legs over the side of the bed. The painted floorboards hurt her feet. She reached for her robe and poked her feet for her bedroom slippers and eased her feet inside.

She found a note from her mother in the kitchen, she was going to go up to help Mrs. Dolan today, and Catherine should find Sheila and walk over to church with her. She made herself some toast and a cup of tea, took it in the living room, and sat in the front windows, feeling like an old lady. She finished eating and drinking, put on her Sunday dress and saddle shoes, her hat, coat, and the beige gloves she wore during Lent, and left the house to find that tall boy, that Paul from last night, standing out on the sidewalk and smoking.

"Hello," he said as she came out, blowing smoke out with the word.

"Hello," she answered. He didn't say anything, and she waited a moment on the top step. "Did you want something?"

"No, I don't want nothing. Your mother met me over up Dolan's and she asked would I wait for you and walk you up church." He looked pleasant and spoke evenly, as he had the other night, but he irritated Catherine the same way.

"Oh, thanks. Thanks anyway. I can go by myself."

"Well, she said she wanted me to go with you."

"So what?" she burst out. "I don't even know you, hardly."

"Well, that's what she said. Suit yourself." He still didn't sound the least bit upset, as if she could come or go for all he cared, she could be as rude as she wanted and it wouldn't bother him.

"Well, I will. You can go chase yourself for all I care."

"Well, maybe I will," he said, and he smiled. "Except I told her I'd stay, and if she asked me I don't know what I'd have to tell her." He took another drag. "But you do what you want."

"You do what you want, too," she said. She shrugged up her shoulders and walked down the steps.

"She said we should stop for your friend Sheila," he said behind her, and she did paused. She didn't think he'd tell on her, but Sheila would. *Oooh, that Sheila*, she thought.

She turned back to him. "You know her?"

"Yeah, I do. Pretty girl."

Was she? Now that he said that, she guessed she was. "She lives up the block. We can stop for her." She included him, but he could stay or follow, as she hoped she was making perfectly clear. He did follow, and they reached the house as a woman was coming out next door, the woman from the park, who stared at Catherine, and stopped at the bottom step to pull something out of her pocketbook, smiling as if to herself, but Catherine felt her face burn even though she was positive the woman had never looked over at her and Paddy.

"Hmph!" Paul said under his breath, and he looked straight ahead toward Sheila's.

"You got a match, sonny?" Carmen said, still rooting in her bag. Paul didn't answer. "Hey! You, boy, you got a match?"

"Yes, I do," he said, not moving or turning his head.

"Well, then, do you want to lend me one?" The way she paused between each word was insulting but funny, too, and Catherine snorted. She winked at her.

Paul extended one hand with a box of matches between his fingers, not looking at her. "There you go," he said. Catherine had never seen a young man talk to a grown woman like that, and coming from this young man it was shocking. Sheila's mother opened the door.

"Oh, hi, honey," she said down to them, "Sheel'll be right out, hon," and she closed the door.

Carmen took out one match, lit her cigarette, and then instead of giving the matches back to Paul, dropped them on the pavement and brought the toe of her high heel shoe down on the match box, and ground the box and the matches into the pavement. She looked fine, as if they weren't there and she was just putting out a lit cigarette. She didn't say another word, walked past them with the strap of her pocketbook on her arm, wrist extended, and crossed the street.

Paul never looked once at her, and now he smiled down at Catherine. Shewas surprised to find herself smiling back at him, and thought as she had last night that he looked really nice, that he had a lovely smile.

Sheila came to the door in her spring coat, brown felt hat, and beige gloves, and as she looked at her, Catherine realized that not only was she pretty, she was exceptionally pretty.

"Hi," she smiled. Sheila didn't answer.

"Sheila, didn't you hear Catherine?" her mother said amiably from behind her where she held the door open.

"Hi," Sheila said.

"Bye, bye, now, girls!" her mother called.

"Don't she go to church?" Paul asked, somewhat irrelevantly, as she thought, but Sheila said right away, "No. She's Luthern."

"Oh, yeah? Me, too. I'm Luthern, too. That's a nice hat you got on, Sheila," Paul replied in his nicest voice, at least the nicest voice Catherine had yet heard him use since he had asked her if she wanted some iced tea, and her hat and Sheila's were exactly the same, they bought them the same place on the same day.

"Don't mind me, I'm all right," she said under her breath as she crossed the street in front of them. On the park side she did begin to feel sick, though. "Let's walk around it," she suggested, but Paul said, "We're late—we'll save a block going through." And he took Sheila's elbow and steered her to the path, and all she could do was follow them like a fool. The wind was cold and brisk, it hurt her body. Her legs still felt leaden, and they were walking straight into the wind, which didn't bother the other two at all, chatting, friendly, Sheila smiling up at Paul, and although they were walking quite fast, they didn't seem out of breath or anything. Catherine couldn't believe that she hadn't known they knew each other.

"Don't you think so?" Sheila smiled back at her, and though she couldn't hear a word they had been saying, she smiled and nodded, and bit her lip.

When they got to the church, Sheila turned and shook Paul's hand.

"Thank you," she said, just like an adult. "I think we can make it back okay ourselves."

"No, that's all right. What is it, about a hour? I'll come back," Paul said.

Catherine knew that if she didn't sit down in one minute, she was going to pass out, so she said, "Goodbye" very quickly, and ran up the steps and into the church. She didn't hear what Sheila said back.

III. Longe a salúte mea verba delictórum meórum

The purple hangings on the altar and the strong odor of incense struck her first, and then the lines of penitents on both sides of the far ends of the pews. The Blessed Sacrament was still open for veneration, meaning they had gotten there faster than she had supposed. She could hear people at the front of church praying the rosary out loud, and when she put her hand out for the holy water to bless herself, it, too, felt icy cold and painful to touch.

"Where you want to sit?" Sheila asked behind her, a little out of breath and smiling.

"I have to go to confession," she said. "I didn't make it yesterday after all. You sit someplace and I'll find you, save me a seat, though, okay?"

Sheila smiled at her again as if Friday had not come between them.

"Oh, sure," she said. "You go head."

Catherine stood in the line, leaning against the wall, saying the prayers of the Stations she stood under as she passed under them. The relief of the painted plaster figures springing as it seemed out of their panels in perpetual activity made each part of the Passion story more real today, and she thought, *You suffered a lot more than I do, but on the other hand, I don't think it lasted quite as long in Your case.*

Maybe if a person's suffering was really extreme, God would make sure they didn't go through it all that long, she thought. Something about that theory sounded fishy to her, but for the moment it helped. As she moved down the confession line, the church filled up, the Rosary finished, the altar boys and the priest fussed over the altar and the candles, genuflecting, silent, comforting to see. There was something about right before Mass started, she couldn't tell you what, but she always loved that time, she loved it now more than ever.

The gentleman ahead of her came out of the confessional and she went in and knelt down. It was hot, and dark, and smelled old, and it felt good to be there until she remembered what she was doing and what she was going to have to say. After probably not much more than two minutes, the priest slid back the small door in the paneling, and she began.

"And what sins have you to confess?" he asked after she asked for his blessing. From the voice and the bad breath she knew it was Fr. Schmidt, who all the girls at school said he could never look at a girl without his ears turning red. She never told him any impure thoughts when she confessed to him, but instead vaguely admitted to lapses in charity and sins of omission which were always easy to come up with. Now she did not know what she was going to do.

"Well, Father. Well, you see, I did something I shouldn't have, and, uh, it made an opportunity for a bigger sin to happen, and, so, even though I didn't do the sin, I probably might have made the person do it." Her palms rested against each other with the fingertips pointing upward, and then she parted them and cleared her throat briefly behind one hand.

"What do you mean?" he asked. "You can't make another person do a sin unless you are sinning also," he continued. "This is especially why marriage was created," he said austerely, in an I-shouldn't-have-to-tell-you-of-all-people tone. He paused, letting that sink in, not, she knew, waiting for any explanation, but then, bizarrely, she worried he might have seen her in the park, too.

"Well?" The voice startled her, and she jumped. "Well," he said again, "What did you do?"

Then she knew she was going to have to lie, and the feeling that the bottom half of her body was about to fall off seemed to be a sign that the pain and burning were sufficient punishment for a sin that two days ago she would not have had the capacity to imagine committing, and all at once she thought, *Oh, this is the penance. So I already have it, and I just need to get the absolution and not lie about it and that's what I'll do.*

"Oh, it wasn't anything like that. I just stuck my tongue out at my friend, and then she stuck hers out at me afterward, and I got really mad and called her a name then."

"Oh? What did you call her?"

"Uh, stupid, I think."

"Well, that's not very charitable is it. It is not a great sin, but anger can always easily lead to a larger one, and I know you don't want that. Don't do it again."

She looked up from her folded hands, and could see through the grate that he was examining his fingernails, holding them straight up. His nails were very nicely shaped, and she was so angry she couldn't tell him the real sin and about him not realizing that it was a lie and a stupid lie into the bargain that she wanted to smack something. "No, Father," she said.

"Is that all you have to confess?"

She assented, recited the closing, not feeling much less heartily sorry. He sighed, another austere and regulated emission, and hearing that sigh, she thought he did know she was lying, and she felt a bit better.

"For your penance, say three Hail Marys, and resolve not to allow your anger to lead another into sin also, however venial," he said.

"No, Father."

Her fingertips trailed automatically to her forehead to imitate and receive the blessing. Still, as the panel door slid shut, darkening the confessional again, she wanted to stay there, but the organ had begun to play. She stepped out and nearly knocked into one of the altar boys heading up the side aisle to the center back to start the processional. It was Micky Stillman, a short little kid in the fifth grade who had a reputation for making other kids laugh at the wrong time and who was grinning at her now, and for some reason she winked at him. As he passed, she could tell from the way his shoulders were hunching up that he was about to crack up, and then Stu Peters followed, a sallow-faced boy who never looked happy except when he was in the small black cassock and laced surplice of the Mass acolyte. His eyes were nearly closed and he looked nearly transfigured. Him she didn't wink at.

Monsignor Abbott followed with the censor, clicking the body of it into the long brass chain, the smoke from the incense so thick it billowed. She had always loved the scent better than anything she could have named, but today it was making her ill, and it, too, like the loud noises, seemed to hurt as she breathed it in, as though the pain were in her brain, not in her nose. As Monsignor reached where she stood in the aisle, pressed lightly back into the velvet curtain of the box she had exited, the music from the organ ceased and the procession stopped.

Monsignor, who was not very tall, was right in front of her, and had she been standing before him her head would have come just under his chin. He was not an easy man, and the screams he let loose when a child didn't follow the order of the Sacrament properly, or when he was outraged at the sin confessed had felled more than one. Now he looked calm and even friendly, and in that moment she wanted to reach her hand out and hold on to the embroidered sleeve of his garment. She contented herself with tracing with her eyes the gold thread that wound around and up the fabric that covered his arm, until she was looking him full in the face. He looked over to her and stretched his mouth in a closed smile. The organ resumed and he took in a breath and stepped forward on the heel of the acolyte who had not been quick enough to move ahead. Monsignor clucked his tongue and the boy shimmied forward, working the heel of his shoe back on to his foot at he walked.

The words of the Introit were now being sung slowly: "Do me justice, O God, and fight my fight against an unholy people, rescue me from the wicked and deceitful man." Catherine stood where she was until the processional reached the front of the church, when she slid to the back wall and stood there, trying to keep from pitching over. Monsignor ascended to the tabernacle, genuflected in the slow and beautiful way that she loved, and spread his arms wide.

The prayers before the first readings seemed to last longer than her legs were going to, but then the congregation finally arrived at the Amen, and those who had seats sank into them. She craned her neck, looking for Sheila but not seeing her, and noticed in the last pew but one there a space for one person, and she went up, motioning to the lady at the end that she would like to come into the pew. Instead of moving down, the woman whipped her knees to the left as Catherine stumbled a genuflection.

"Honest to truth," the lady muttered under her breath.

Catherine seemed to be seeing the entire interior of the church where she might never have been. The backs of the heads in front of her stood out strangely, the wrinkles on the sunburned necks of the men, the wisps of hair coming out underneath the pillbox hats of the women, marring what would have been per-fect uptwists of hairdos, the tops of the heads of the smaller kids trying not to mess around in the pews. It must have clouded over completely outside, for it was quite dark now and the lights and candles cast a muted light like the twilight in winter you might see stepping down off a streetcar. She looked up at the painted figures in the apse, where Mary, her arms outstretched, her foot perpetually crushing a snake underneath, had lifted her eyes to the painting of Jesus above her.

"Come down to me," Catherine prayed under her breath with a suddenness that she hadn't intended and didn't expect. "Holy Mary, Mother of God, pray for us sinners, now and at the hour of our death." She closed her eyes and squeezed them tightly, the balls of light left behind inside her eyelids like the stars do at the end of the world.

"Come down to me, Holy Mother of God," she prayed again.

And then she felt Paddy Dolan's thing burning heavy in her hand as she prayed, and she clutched her fist together as if to make no room for it, but it felt as if she were squeezing Paddy instead of her own flesh. She opened her palm and turned it over on one leg, where it burned into the already-hot thigh under her plaid skirt. There was no place to put her hand.

She opened her eyes to find the church just the same, Mary's immaculately conceived self still painted to the ceiling, and Catherine just another girl who had been stupid and had something disgusting happen to her. That's all that it was. That had to be all it was.

IV. Et egréssus foras, flevit amáre.

She kept her eyes shut as the long Gospel of the Passion began.

"Crucify him!" the priest intoned. "I find no fault in this man," he said in the voice of Pilate. It was just the same as it had ever been: a formula, a foregone conclusion: a package of information you could do nothing with but bow down in awe to and feel ashamed about for the rest of your life.

The congregation had been standing all this while but she had remained sitting with her eyes shut. Her defection was apparently too much for the girdled lady, who finally leaned down to her as if she were her own kid and shook her by the arm, whispered, "Psst! Are you sick?"

Catherine opened her eyes. "No, ma'am, I'm fine."

"Well, then, stand on up!"

She stood for a minute, and then she couldn't anymore. She plumped down on the pew with a kind of flop, and looked up at the woman. "I'll be all right."

"Fffffff!" the woman said through her teeth, gave up on her, and turned back around.

Monsignor said, "Blood and water poured from his side," and then she knew she had to get out, that this pain was going to get very bad, and she felt the blood collecting, too, and wondered whether it had already soaked through her dress and her coat, how much there was, how she could get back home this way.

Mommy, she thought, and then, *Just wait, Paddy Dolan, you better wish you never see me again. You better.* It became a prayer there where she sat, to the continued obvious fury of the lady, who when she glanced Catherine noted was wearing way too much lipstick, and that it had started to melt down the lines next to her mouth. She had on a lot of face powder, too, filling up a complexion full of pock marks, and then she felt sorry, because maybe the lady had had smallpox, and maybe had been in an iron lung or something, or had a limp. She was pretty fat, though, so maybe not.

When the woman finally sat down for the Offertory, as the collection plate went around, Catherine whispered to her in the most polite voice she could muster, "Miss, I have to get up and go. I think I am sick."

"You just sit there and think about what you've done till Church is out, now," she whispered back in a voice as void of sympathy as Monsignor Abbot's had ever been.

Catherine slumped back into the pew. *Maybe I could become a nun*, she thought, although as she said this she was fairly sure that if you had held a man's thing the convent would not let you in, for sure not if you sat in church before God and the Blessed

Mother vowing to do terrible things to the person who had put his thing in your hand because you had been so stupid as to sit next to him outside in the dark. She bet they didn't even let you in if you got your time of the month. She didn't know that they got theirs. She wouldn't have thought so. She bet they made you tell them everything, though, and either way, she would be out before she even got in.

Catherine remained sitting in the pew, not even having put her penny in the collection basket, until it was time for her row to go to communion. The lady stepped back to let her out in front of her, exactly as if she had been her mother making sure she didn't make for the door. She walked slowly up the aisle, the way they had taught them to do for their Confirmation, hearing the lady's heavy breathing behind her, until the woman hissed, "Move it along!" and she hurried it up, a little. When she knelt at the altar railing the cold marble cut into her knees and her wrists. Then one of the priests came to her and held up the host before her.

"*Corpus Christi*," he said.

Catherine lifted her head and stuck out her tongue, her hands folded and pointed to heaven under her chin, her eyes closed. The server placed the host perfectly and firmly in the center of her tongue, as if he knew by the look on her face she was one of the ones who would likely let it fall out of her mouth and to the ground otherwise. She pulled her tongue in as her head bowed, placed one hand across her breast as the other lifted her to her feet, and barely touched the floor as she went back up the aisle, past the last pew but one and out the front doors of the church, with the many fathers and other men who had fulfilled their obligation and now needed a smoke, and who looked up at her as if they were all in a tavern and she was one of their daughters who had wandered in behind them.

Paul was standing at the bottom of the steps, smoking. He looked up and smiled when he saw her.

"No!" she cried then, and all the men looked at her first, and then at him like he was about to do something awful. She tapped furiously down the steps, holding her coat around her, turned away from all of them, and ran on her toes down the street to home.

When she got there, she ran up to the bathroom right away. She yanked up her coat and skirt, pulled down her underpants, and sank into the open toilet seat. She leaned over, pressing her hot stomach into her thighs, peered into the sanitary pad, and found a massive collection of blood and that liver-looking stuff that always accompanied it the first couple of days, which she also had not mentioned to her mother or anyone, not really knowing what it might be except hoping it wasn't anything that would kill you.

Daggone, you are stupid. She wanted her mother, and she couldn't stand the thought of her. The porcelain of the toilet seat hurt her the same way all that sound in church and the wind out on the street had, she couldn't get away from it and it didn't feel good the way cold ought to on hot skin. She flushed, sat back down, and started to cry. And then the words she knew she didn't speak, and if she had spoken them she would not at all have known to whom she was saying them, cascaded unspoken and she could not have told you to whom she said them: *Do you love me?* And of whom she wished an answer, she didn't know.

There was a washrag lying over the rim of the bathtub, and she stood and reached for it, and leaned over to the sink and turned the hot water on, wetted the rag as well as she could, and turned the water off before she wiped between her legs. She picked her way over to the cupboard and found a pad and put it on. She thought if she went downstairs and tried to sit in the window in one of the big chairs that would all right, that it would be comfortable, and warmer, so she did that, but the slight draft coming in through the window felt dreadful, and even the upholstery of the chair that she had always found soft and comforting was now harsh and painful to her skin. She was hungry but nothing sounded good. She went to the kitchen, found a dinner roll left over from supper last night, bit into it. It was stale and tasted like soap. She spit the bite out into her hand, threw it into the garbage pail, rinsed her mouth out with some water, thought, *I'll go to Woolworth's and get some more pads and some Midol,* which she had never taken before but thought that if nothing else she could read the box to figure out how you took it. *Probably just like aspirin.*

She had naturally found Woolworth's closed, which, she thought, if she had a brain left in her head she would have known it would be on Sunday, and then, after crying out on the sidewalk in front of the locked door of the store for about five minutes until some people walked by and stared at her as if she didn't have good sense, walked farther along in the same direction, away from home, until she reached a little corner store that happened to be open. She went inside, and there was a small man with a beard and wearing the black cap she had seen before and always called a man's chapel veil.

"What is it?"

She didn't know how to ask for what she needed exactly. "Is your wife here?" she asked him. "I need something for my mother."

"Medicine?" he asked shortly.

"No, sir."

"Never mind," he said, and got up off his stool and reached for the claw that picked items off the top shelves. He moved to the back wall, where there was a small array of Kotex boxes in a location he would not have been able to see them from had he glanced up to the top shelves from his seat. He picked off a box, let it drop into his arm, brought it to the counter without looking at her, asked, "Do you have a bag?" and when she said no, ripped off a sheet of butcher paper from the big roll next to him and wrapped the box up and tied it with string as if it were a pot roast or a chicken. She liked the look of that, and determined that she might always buy Kotex pads from this man at this store on Sundays, as ridiculous as that might be.

He resumed reading his paper. "How much?" she asked, and he called out to the back room in a language she didn't understand. A woman's voice answered, and he told her the price. She held the money out to him, but he acted as if she were not there and so she put the money down on the counter, although her mother had taught her that was very rude and she didn't like to do it. He looked over his paper at that, though, and snorted.

"Can't win for losing," she said, as she thought to herself, but he smiled then, and she realized she had said it out loud.

"You know what day it is?" he asked her.

"Sunday?" she said.

"Palm Sunday, this is what you call it, yes?"

"Oh. Yes."

"I keep the store open on Sunday."

"Oh."

"Oh," he repeated. "This is the only word you know?"

She didn't answer.

"All right, go home now. I'm going to close. What are you doing here anyway? But I suppose in the case of illness that would be different." He paused, smiled again, seemed to think the better of that, and said again, "Go on, now."

V. *Líbera me de ore leónis: et a córnibus unicórnium humilitátem meam*

I should just go home, she thought out on the pavement, looking at up the "Closed" sign in the door window. The walk back was still cold and the sun hurt. She passed beside the park again and looked in to see if anybody was there, but it appeared to be empty of everything but what littered the sidewalks and the paths. The few early spring flowers that there were looked as if they were trying to find a way back into the ground, and though the sun was shining again, the air was so bitter that it took all her will to keep from crying out. She didn't spend a second considering knocking on Sheila's door. She stepped off the curb and walked over to the square side, and went in, walking the diagonal of it as she had done on the way to Mass. When she reached the far corner, she stood a moment gazing at the grey exterior of the House of Good Shepherd, and then looked across the block at all of the beautiful houses on Hollins Street. Why they seemed better to her, brighter and nicer-looking, she couldn't say. Maybe it was the way the sun hit them almost all day, but of all the places that she could have lived besides her own house, she dreamed of living here. With a butler, maybe, and a car. It was funny how one little place could seem like somewhere so different, but it was that way. Every time you turned a corner, you were in another neighborhood, maybe with a different style of house, maybe in the same world, but maybe too in a different one.

"Oh, that's where I left it," someone said behind her. It was Carmen, who bent down to a nearby bench to pick up a brown paper bag that clearly held a bottle. She looked up, saw her, and laughed.

"That's all right. I don't care if you have some. Take a drink if you want." She held out the bottle toward her, but Catherine shook her head. "I don't think I know who you are," she said then.

"I'm Catherine Bernstein. Um, sorry, I was just going home. Were you—did you need something?"

Carmen just laughed. "No," she said, "I thought you were someone else. I'm Carmen, I know Miss Maurice," she said, and then she belched in what Catherine thought was a very charming way, blowing her cheeks out just a little and putting her fist up to her mouth. She laughed. "I'm Carmen," she said again. "I know Miss Maurice. You know her?"

"I know her some, I mean, I think I've heard her name."

Carmen belched again. "Excuse me!" she laughed. "You do, do you?"

"Yes, I think so. Maybe I do. I'm not real sure," she said, embarrassed now and irritated. This was all just foolish, she thought.

"No kidding," Carmen said, and then as Catherine blushed, "Never mind. You're all right. For a white girl."

"What do you mean?" she asked, looking at her sharply. She didn't like how she said that at all, but wasn't she white? Catherine would have sworn that she was.

"Oh, I don't know," Carmen said. "I got dumped by this white boy once. Who did he think he was, dumping me? I was a catch. And he was a roly-poly, too. Nothing to look at, I promise you."

She sat down on the bench and for a minute didn't say anything more. Catherine liked the way she looked, and if she was colored, she realized that she liked the way she didn't seem to act like it, though it made her a little nervous, but she didn't know what for. Her hair was short, and dark, and curled all over her head like a little boy's, but it was soft, too, and gleamed. She wasn't very tall, not as tall as her, and otherwise small all around with a really big bosom that was visible under her open spring coat. Catherine had begun to make a habit of noticing bosoms and wondering how hers would turn out. Even so, she was impressed with Carmen's arms, tight and muscular like a man's, and her eyebrows, tracing the thinnest line above her eyes Catherine had ever seen, but not gaudy or with the constantly surprised expression so many ladies had when they plucked them like that. She wore a plain white blouse and a full, dark-colored skirt, but on her mouth was a great big streak of red lipstick the color of which, whenever she saw it on someone out on the street, her mother would say, "Uh-oh." Catherine didn't know exactly what that meant, but she was enjoying talking to someone who would have made her mother make that noise. With what she knew about Carmen, her mother would have had a lot more to say than "Uh-oh," and she sure wouldn't have been saying it to her. She thought probably Carmen had actually broken the law with that man on Friday night. She shuddered, and held the package tighter as if the difficulty were merely the wind. She searched for something else to say

"Why do you drink beer in the middle of the day?" she asked.

Carmen burst out laughing. "I don't know—doesn't everybody? I wish I had some whiskey, but I don't have any whiskey in the house." She looked around, as if she might find some sitting on a shelf out there in the park. "Besides, it probably is too early for whiskey. I can't get loaded yet. I have a date later. With a man. Not Mr. Morris, Mr. Gailes." She was quiet for a moment, and then said, "Hey. You want to see something?"

Catherine shrugged. "Sure," she said.

"Okay, c'mere and sit down."

She did, and Carmen unbuttoned the two top buttons of her blouse, and then pulled the collar aside and leaned over. "Look at that," she said.

Just under her collar bone next to the strap of her slip there was a kind of raised and pebbly looking mark. Part of it was red, part of it black, making the shape of a tiny lizard with a long tail and what could be taken for four legs, but a flat straight edge where the head of the animal might be if it were an actual lizard. It looked more like a scab than anything, but it didn't look temporary.

"What is it?"

"It's the mark of the devil. The devil's in there," she said, and winked. Catherine pulled back, and Carmen laughed.

"Can't you get rid of it?" Catherine asked.

"Nope. I was born with it. That's why I'm special. That's why I'm always special," she said.

"But doesn't it hurt?"

"Nope," she said again, buttoning up. "It itches sometimes, but that's about it."

"But, I mean, does it really put the devil in you?"

"Yes, ma'am," she said. "But I don't care. That's the great thing about it. You never have to care, about anything. Everything you do is exactly what you want to do. The only thing that would make a difference would be if I went to the church and had the priest throw holy water on it. Then the devil couldn't use it anymore."

"Oh. Well, how do you know that?"

"I just do."

She turned her head and Catherine looked at her profile from where she stood, and then she saw it as it had lain against the man's chest. If that man, the one she'd been with, had been Mr. Gailes, he had certainly looked like he could be the devil, or someone the devil knew pretty well.

Carmen said, sort of peering at her, "What is it? Don't you like to talk about the devil, or what?"

"No, no, it's nothing like that. I just don't feel too good," she answered, happy to have an excuse for whatever it was Carmen had seen on her face.

"Too bad. Not catching, is it?"

Catherine smiled then, and looked away. That was the first thing she had found funny since waking up this morning, which also now seemed as if it had been months ago. "No. No, it's nothing catching," she said.

She looked over again to the House of Good Shepherd, saw one of the sisters closing the shades in the front window, and said, "I think I'd like to go in there one day," and when Carmen didn't answer she looked down at her. She was staring straight ahead, and looked both angry and afraid. "What?" she said. "Don't you like it?"

Carmen looked up then, and laughed, and said, "Whew! Lord, God, I would hate going into that house. How you can stand to even think about it!"

"What do you mean? I think I would like it there, mostly. You know, quiet and all clean and everything. Wouldn't you like it there?"

"God, no." Carmen seemed to use the Lord's name in vain without thinking about it, but it didn't sound like swearing, it sounded like she was on a first-name basis with the Almighty, Who was maybe somebody she wouldn't give two cents for. "God damn, I wouldn't be able to wait to get out of that place if I ever had to go in it. Don't talk to me about that place!"

"Well, how come?"

Carmen stood up and yanked her by the arm, talked right into her face: "I *said* don't talk to me about it!" She peered down the street then and said, "We should go somewhere. You want to go somewhere?" She made it sound like a question, but kept Catherine's elbow in her wiry fist.

"No. No, I don't want to go with you!" Catherine nearly screamed it, and then she could feel her hand burn again as if Paddy Dolan's thing were in it again. She started to cry, pulling away as if Carmen had struck her or was trying to force her into a car. Carmen dropped her arm immediately but Catherine stayed, the tears heavy on her face, staring at her but not running away.

"What's the big deal?" Carmen said, smiling. "I just thought — you know, it's Sunday. We should go out, go do something."

Then Catherine knew she didn't want to go home at all. Carmen sort of smirked, sort of chuckled at her, in a way that might have told Catherine that her thoughts floated across her face for anyone to read, but Carmen didn't say that. She said, "What's the big deal?" again, and then, peering across over to

Hollins herself, "I just had an idea. Let's go downtown. I've got some friends on Charles Street. You want to? I'll get you home in time, no big deal."

"Sure, okay," Catherine said, smiling, wondering what in the world she was doing and hoping that neither Sheila nor Sheila's mother were looking out of their house over at them. "Sure, why not?" she said again, and even smiled back.

"Great," Carmen said, smiling back. "Have a drink," she said, holding out the bottle, and Catherine had one and whatever it was, because it wasn't beer, it didn't even make her splutter.

They walked a while down Hollins toward the Market until they came to a call box, and Carmen called for a cab. Catherine mouthed to her that she didn't have any money, but she just shook her head at her and finished the call. "It's not too much," she said. "I can manage it." And once they got into the taxi, all the way down she chatted about it seemed like every living thing, all the boyfriends she had had, her husband, Mr. Morris, whom she had married when she had gotten pregnant, "in the family way," when she had just been sixteen, and how she went by Stunchen, which she confided was a name she had invented, but that her two daughters were both named Morris and that Mr. Morris would be the father of all of her children.

"Yeah, he comes around every few years just to knock me up," she said, as casually as if she was describing the visit of a census taker or a funeral home director. "Speak of the devil, though, I'm feeling a little woozy my own self. But, you know, that's life."

VI. *Dinumeraverunt omnia ossa mea ipsi vero consideraverunt et inspexerunt me*

The cab ride downtown was fast compared to how long it took the busses and the street car, and in no time they turned up Charles Street, and then in another few blocks it seemed, pulled up in front of a row of houses whose front doors were high up off the sidewalk, practically on the second floor, and whose steps reached out over the pavement and partly covered the basements below, businesses mostly, a beauty parlor, and a couple of plain doors. There was music coming out of the window of one of them and as they walked up the white marble steps, she felt a thrill that made her think of Petie.

And then she felt a little woozy, and then after that, she could afterward remember Carmen's hand on the front door, turning it, and smiling down at her and saying, "Come on up," but not much of anything until waking and finding herself sitting on the floor of a house she knew she had never been in before. A fat white woman dressed in nothing but a black slip that she guessed was nearly large enough to use as the sheet on Catherine's bed was taking up the majority of a sofa, and she was drinking soda out of a bottle. A young man, very thin and very black, dressed in slacks and a belt, with a sleeveless t-shirt tucked into them, came up to the woman and laughed down at her.

"Oh, Miss Edna," he said, "You don't look too good."

"Hush up," Miss Edna said. "I was feeling poor and getting better before you was ever born, son."

The man grinned and looked over at Catherine. "What she doing here?"

"Don't you mind her, and don't you mess with her, neither. She's Carmen's."

"What's Carmen got to bring her around here for anyway?"

"What does Carmen do anything for? I don't understand that woman and I don't think I ever will."

"Somebody ought to clean her up." He jerked his head at Catherine.

Miss Edna snorted. "I ain't working on Sunday. Let her clean herself up."

Catherine's head started to buzz. It was still Sunday, that wasn't the problem, she knew it was Sunday, but what time was it? She couldn't feel her body, saw her legs sticking straight out, one bent at a right angle underneath the other, the backs of her ankle socks down into the heels of her shoes, now, she saw, not saddle shoes but penny loafers that fit loosely on her feet. She only had one pair of shoes, and though this year her mother said she might add a pair of shoes with a bit of a heel for Easter, but now, seeing the loafers, she couldn't recall how she had come by them, didn't mind that they were a bit too large, and thought that if she never found out whose they were and had to give them back, she would not trade them for all the high-heeled shoes in the universe.

On this thought she bent, turned to the side, and was sick on the floor, heaving strangely and insistently. When the paroxysm was over, she leaned back into the wall. "Why am I upchucking?" she asked, looking up at the lady.

"Don't ask me," she said. "Carmen must have give you something disagreed with you."

Who is Carmen? she thought, and then, *I don't want to go with you,* but she knew she wasn't saying that to this lady. Apart from that, she didn't feel like she could move much at all. There were a couple of soda crackers on the floor next to her on the other side and she remembered that crackers were good for you if you were throwing up, and she picked one up and slowly brought it up to her mouth, having to aim the one to get to the other, and bit into it. The young man laughed out loud, said, "Look at her! Eating crackers right off the floor!" and the large woman opened her legs slightly to hunch forward and sit up a little straighter on the sofa, and Catherine could smell her, thick and flat, a smell that couldn't be ignored or gotten past and filled the room. She didn't get sick this time, but didn't dare open her mouth. She stared at the cracker until she wanted to put it behind her and pretend it had never been, but knew she couldn't.

"Oh, my Lord," Miss Edna said, "Carmen brought us a winner this time." And everybody laughed, and Catherine laughed a little bit herself, and the woman smiled at her with what seemed like some approval.

"I'm going to tell you a story," she said then. She looked at Catherine, nodded, and Catherine tried to look away but couldn't. Miss Edna had three chins easily and what looked to be four rolls of stomach that seemed to have been sewn on to her body. "That's right," she said, as if reading Catherine's thoughts, "I didn't used to always be this size. I used to be a little flower stem of a thing, swaying in the breeze, knock me over with a feather." She cackled then. "And that is just what happened."

"I was born in Highlandtown, my father had been in the slaughterhouses when he was a young man, we liked it over there, except, you know, the smells and all. I didn't think I'd ever move, but we had to after while, because I kept getting the croup and my lungs were just about wore out...."

People Catherine had never seen before kept wandering in and out of the room as the lady continued her story, most of which she could not make out at all, except that she seemed to have had an astonishing number of beaux, whom she valued in direct proportion to the elaborate nature of the dinners or the crab feasts or the beer hall sojourns they would take her to, and how when it came time for the romantic portion of the evening, she was always too full to kiss them. Sometimes people would stare into Catherine's face, looking concerned or laughing, and other times they didn't seem to know she was there.

"And then we moved over here, to this very house, with my father and my mother and my six sisters and two brothers. But I was always the prettiest one, and I always had good beaux in those years."

She looked down at her massive body, smoothed her slip. "I lost both brothers in the war, did I tell you that? Both of them. One dysentery and one got blown up in Belgium by somebody. They don't know exactly. So we buried one of them but we put both markers on. Our folks had up and died already.

"I didn't marry. Did I tell you that? Well, I couldn't. Nobody liked him but me. My sisters wouldn't have nothing to do with him, and my brothers would have killed him, taken him out and killed him with a shotgun. But I loved him. He worked at the Armory, swept up and cleaned the restrooms and all that. Good job. And then it changed over here and that was fine, but he left. He said he couldn't stand for no three hundred pound white woman shaking his bed to bits at night," and she laughed, and the young man, still standing there, laughed loud and hard.

VII. Omnes videntes me deriserunt me locuti sunt labiis moverunt caput

Someone came in then, said, "Hey, Miss Edna!" and turned on the record player again. The music began to play and more people wandered in and stayed, dancing in couples, men and women, girls and girls, some of them just moving to the music by themselves, snapping their fingers, humming. Catherine wanted to get up and join them but she still couldn't get herself up off the floor. An older woman came to her with a bucket and began to mop up where she had gotten sick, and at the scent of the ammonia in the bucket Catherine actually felt a little better, but she could still hardly move. A little boy came into the room as the woman finished up, he walked up to Catherine, climbed up on her lap, and put his head on her chest. She was able to put her arms around him and then tried to pat him, but though her arms were tingling now, she couldn't coordinate them, so she just held him while he sucked his thumb and rested his head under her chin.

The record stopped, and at that moment two people she recognized very well walked into the room. Paddy Dolan was with Carmen, and she remembered coming to this place with her. They were laughing, Paddy very free with her, kissing her on the face and slapping her bottom, laughing and talking to her as if they were the only two people in the room, until he looked around and saw Catherine, who stiffened, and the little boy whimpered a bit, as if he could feel he was going to have to move soon. Catherine tried to glare at Paddy, but it turned out that all she could do was laugh. Paddy looked angry, then ugly, and he let go of Carmen and walked over to Catherine and stooped down to her.

"Let's get you home, Niamh," he said sternly, as if he were her father.

Catherine found this even funnier than anything else so far. "Neeve!" she said, looking up at him. "I'm a neeve!" And she burst out laughing so loud that another few people from the inner room came out, and everyone else laughed with her, and the little boy jumped up and started to cry as if she had told him she was going to take him to the orphanage, after which another woman came over and swatted him one, and he stopped crying and the tears rolled down his skin, leaving a trail of white salt.

Carmen came over, reached down and took Paddy by the arm, shaking it. She leaned over, too, bit his ear, whispered to him, but he ignored her, and stared at Catherine hard in turn, and then he grinned.

Something about all of this must have brought Catherine back to life, because she started feeling better by the minute, even all at once, and far from wanting to give it to Paddy, she thought he was about the funniest thing she had ever seen. Then she was up on her feet, saying, "I want a dance!" and somebody said, "Sure, baby, let's dance," and took her hand while everyone else laughed and talked. It was a very nice-looking colored boy who held led her on to the floor and held her hand and started to spin her around. She had no idea what she was doing, but it was fun, and she soon got the hang of most of the steps. She liked the way the boy looked and how he smelled, like violets, and she liked the smooth slick curling of his hair on his head like a wig, thick and perfectly cascading in waves from his tan brow to his neck. His teeth were yellow from smoking, and the whites of his eyes seemed both very white and more bloodshot than she had noticed anyone's eyes to be before. He had thin lips and a thin nose in a wide, square face, and he was tall and slender. She never learned his name or met him again, but she remembered later thinking he was so pretty. As she danced, she decided she was going to find out what this place was and come back again, and then she thought maybe she might even stay here forever, if the white lady in the black slip would let her.

The boy swung her around hard all at once and she managed not to fall, and she called out, "We're doing good!" and he laughed. People made room for them, and she looked over to Carmen, and to Paddy, who wasn't looking at her at all, but staring down at the fat woman on the couch with an expression on his face as if he couldn't believe what he was seeing.

Then the music stopped all at once, and she and the boy stopped a moment after, and she held on to the boy's arm so as not to fall down, and he leaned into her for a kiss, but she leaned away and said, "Uh-uh!"

"Have it your way," he said, but still smiling, and he let her go and moved over to the table and began to eat something.

VIII. *Aperuerunt super me os suum sicut leo rapiens et rugiens*

The big lady was still telling the story of her life but aside from her voice the room had settled down into unselfconscious noises and small conversations, and most of the people were eating or drinking quietly. Catherine felt a little bit hungry and moved over to the table next to the boy, who handed her a plate and a cloth napkin. She started to thank him when Paddy's voice cut across the room.

"Jesus, Carmen, why do you have to hang around with a bunch of niggers like this?" he said, loud but casually, as if nobody could hear him, but still looking straight at Miss Edna. Then everything but the music stopped, and the boy stepped away from Catherine, squinted and shook his head.

Miss Edna rose to her feet, which took a great deal of doing, but once she was up, she commanded the room. "Excuse me?" she spat at Paddy. "What did you just say?"

Paddy looked at her as if he was astonished to be addressed at all, as if she hadn't been an actual person but some kind of a talking story machine, part of a book that had come to life there on the sofa. He looked down at his broken hand, seemed to be wondering what he ought to do with it.

"I beg your pardon, madam," he said after a moment, in a tone of voice that Catherine knew well, but still could not figure out from what part of him it must come. "I spoke a thought aloud."

"Don't give me that crapola," Edna said. "I've had it up to here with people like you. Up to here. Get out of my house, take your doped-up little friend with you"—she pointed to Catherine—"and don't let me see your face in my house again."

She spit down on her own floor, and several of the other people standing there said some variation of "Uh-huh." Paddy looked at her again for a moment with that look Catherine had also seen before, that she knew meant he was having trouble figuring out who Edna was, and then his face looked very tender, and he said, "Of course, the child is unwell. Thank you, madam, for your kindness in reminding me. I'll take her home at once."

"No!" Catherine said at that, surprising even herself. "I don't want to go with him!" She tried to hold her hand out to the boy, but he acted as if she were not there, and moved away from her as quietly and slowly as he could.

Miss Edna didn't look at her, nor, did it seem, anyone else except Carmen, who looked angry and frightened, and it occurred to Catherine that she would not have thought Carmen ever felt fear. "Don't give me that," Miss Edna said to Paddy. "Look, I'm not going to say it again. Get out of my house and take that girl with you."

Catherine wanted to cry out again, say, *No, I'm not going with you, you're not my mother*, but she knew she didn't say the words out loud. She twisted her body toward the boy, her face turned into the wall, and there was a long pause when nobody moved or spoke until finally one of the ladies said, "Miss Edna, I know this is your house, but I don't think she want to go with that man. Maybe she shouldn't go with him, Miss Edna."

"Give her to Carmen," Miss Edna said, and Catherine could hear in her voice that she was bored with everything. The last thing she said was, "As long as you get them out of my house, I don't care what happens to them." She eased herself back down into the sofa, but still no one else moved, and it seemed that nobody really knew what to do, including Paddy. But Carmen finally walked over and took Catherine's arm just as she had done in the park, and said between her teeth, "Why, hello, baby, come on with me," and steered her upstairs.

Catherine's hat, coat, and gloves were sitting on a bed, waiting for her, as if this were the home of someone she would visit any day, at any time, and she knew the people who lived here well, she was attached to them in some way, she was of their kind, of their family. That was how she felt for a moment, but now she knew she wasn't remotely one of them. The bedspread itself was covered in a riot of very faded and ugly flowers, and the brown of her coat next to it looked like the earth out of which they had sprung, but as strange as this thought was, she was that much of a stranger in the house, and she felt not so much sad at thinking this as empty. Carmen helped her into her things, for once not saying a word but peering at her as if she expected Catherine to say something to her. When Catherine didn't speak, Carmen finally put the package, obviously opened and re-wrapped and tied in the paper and string, into her hands, and yanked her down the stairs.

"Thanks for nothing," she said to Paddy when they reached the bottom. "Take her on home now."

"So I'll be by later to your place?" he said in reply.

"Suit yourself. I don't give a care," Carmen said, and went back into the party without giving either of them another look.

Paddy pulled Catherine by the elbow out of the house and out on to the street. He looked up and down, but there were no cars on the street then, no taxis.

He seemed defeated. "Go home with you, now, girl," he said. And he shook his head again, as if he were clearing something out of his mind. She tried to move, but had no idea where she was but that she must be somewhere near downtown, this place looked a little bit like that, and she recalled remarking the odd steps that came out over the basement entrances of the block when they had come in. She didn't feel light anymore, but sick, her head pounding with something insistent she didn't know how to fix. She didn't move.

"All right, then, come with me," Paddy said.

"No!" she cried out. "I'm not going with you!"

"Don't be a little fool," he said. "You can't walk home by yourself. At least let me get you over to Baltimore and put you on a street car."

"No," she said again, not believing him, wishing she were somewhere else, with her cousins, with Petie, even with Paul. "No, I'm not going to," she said, but weakly, and she knew she had to.

He took her arm. "You're coming along with me, Niamh," he said and she did not resist.

They passed building after building, house after house, sometimes with people out on their steps, standing in overcoats, walking on the sidewalks, not looking at them, Paddy holding on to her arm, her feet flopping in those penny loafers, him threatening under his breath every now and again what he'd do to her if she tried to run or cry out, she in her mind answering him with terrible vengeance, she didn't understand why he was talking to her that way, and though she was afraid, she felt tight and closed in. All she wanted was to get his voice out of her ear. She flinched every time he spoke, reminding her of what had happened to Petie, gripping her arm and pulling her.

The street car could be seen not many blocks down when they reached Baltimore Street, and there Paddy pulled some money out of his trousers pocket, put it in her hand, said, "You go straight home, now. You don't ever mention this to anyone. You don't ever tell anyone anything," and she didn't know if he meant today, or the night before, or that he'd said the word "nigger" in the presence of colored people, or that they'd been with Carmen, or all of it.

And she turned to him and said, "I don't need your money."

And then he leaned into her, very close, and his breath smelled like green onions and horseradish.

"Let me go," she said, starting to cry. "You get your cotton-picking hands off me, Paddy Dolan," she said, and he laughed, a genuine laugh, and looked as he had on Friday afternoon when she had first thought she loved him.

"Let yourself go," he said, and then he put his mouth on her. It was not a kiss. She didn't know what to call it. The smell, like those things, the onions and horseradish and maybe whiskey or beer, and maybe beef or something else that was sour and powerful, hurt almost as much as his hand on her arm, and then his tongue was round and full between her lips, and she gagged and made a retching motion and pulled her mouth away, the short stubble on his face cutting into her skin. He didn't seem to mind, and he didn't let her go, and though he laughed at her he didn't come in for anything more, either.

"Let yourself go, darling Niamh," he not quite whispered. "You'll want to see me again, I can tell you that much. I'll be here when you're ready, too, darlin Niamh. I'll be here for you, you know I will."

He swept his bad hand over the top of her head, letting it linger in her hair, his eyes covering her face. Then he dropped her arm, shoved the car fare in her hand, and walked away. When the street car was almost at the stop she heard a low, long whistle, and turned again where Paddy had been. He stood maybe a half a block away, raised his hand, and waved.

"Goodbye, Niamh! Goodbye!"

IX. Tenuísti manum déxteram meam : et in voluntáte tua deduxísti me : et cum glória assumpsísti me.

She swung into her seat, stared into her face in the window glass, and through it to the buildings and stores and gasoline stations moving past. All she could feel was that tongue of his between her lips, smelted into them, rough and limp and cold and wet all at the same time. What if he was right? What if she ever had to see him again, talk to him again, and she shivered, said to herself, *No!* but his thing was in her hand and his tongue was in her mouth, and she didn't think she might ever get them out. She hadn't known what it felt like to be terrified, she'd had bad dreams and some nightmares, but this was something else all over again, and she shook in the seat, unable to control it or to calm it down. She looked out the window, saw her face in the window glass, and saw that she looked just the same as she had a couple of days ago, though her bangs were straighter, but even so she felt as if she couldn't quite place the face that she saw. It was too old, maybe, then not old enough, then light, then dark, then pretty, then hideous, then wizened, then twice the size.

But then something happened that when she looked back later she couldn't fully understand. She began to think of Sheila, and her mother and Paul, and Petie, and for a moment she felt happy, back to herself. She thought of the painting of Mary on the apse of St. Martin's, and then she thought, *I'll tell Petie every-thing*, and then she thought, *No, I won't tell him a thing. I'll just keep it to myself*, not as if he wasn't someone she could tell anything to, but that this was something different between them, and she had never felt such separation from him before. It wasn't as if he wasn't really hers at all, it wasn't that. It was something more like, all that no longer had anything to do with this minute.

And then she felt Paddy's breath on her face again, and his hand on her arm, and she thought, *Well, that's what you get.*

She exited the streetcar at Stricker and walked slowly down from Baltimore toward Union Square and home, thinking over and over, *That's what you get. That's what you get.* It didn't bother her, though: it felt a little lonely, and when things about Paddy crept in she was frightened, but then she would look at something, a step railing or a street lamp, and it would become now, and Paddy had happened, but it didn't matter that he had happened. It was getting dark out and plenty of windows with the lights on in them, and, passing not quite under the windows of the front rooms where in one a man listened to a radio, a couple of chil-dren played with toys in another, a woman called out a question in another, she was at home again, home at Union Square where nothing could hurt her and nothing could change her.

All the furniture in every window was the same, the wall-papers the same, the scents and moods and quiet and noise all just the same. It was chilly, getting colder, but the wind had died out and the night air was lovely, and she wasn't nervous to walk alone at all. She looked into Sheila's front window, where there was a lamp on but no one in the front room, and she felt something like a deep love for her, her best friend, who was pretty and good and who might be an idiot after all, but who cared about that, and anyway, she wasn't.

Her head had cleared from whatever it was that she had taken at Miss Edna's, she could walk just fine. She looked over to the square and stopped again, considering it, wanting something there that she knew wasn't there, but maybe it would be once, sometime, and everyone would like it just as she did.

When she crossed Lombard, just past the VFW hall she saw a cab pull up in front of Petie's house, the door opened at the curb, and she saw him get out of it, very slowly, holding on to the frame of the door and pulling himself up with his sound hand. He said something she couldn't hear and the cab driver got out and came around, helped him on to the sidewalk, shut his door, and took him by the arm. She walked a little bit more quickly, called out, "Hi, Petie," and though the cab driver looked over to her, he didn't.

"Which one's his, miss?" the man said.

"It's right here," she said, "It's one-thirteen."

"Could you knock on it for me?" he said, but as he did, Petie's mother and father came out, and gathered him up like a little boy.

"Oh, Pete, oh Pete!" his mother said. "We were so worried! We didn't know what had happened to you!" She saw her, and said, "Oh, Catherine! Did you find him, honey? Oh, thank you!"

Petie's dad didn't say anything, as usual, but she was close enough to see his face suffused with strong feeling and tears on his cheeks. He tried to pay the cab driver, who said, "No, sir, them other people took care of it and I got what I need," at which Petie's dad gave her a speaking look and patted her on the arm.

They took Petie into the house, and the door slammed shut behind them. The cab driver said goodnight to her, and drove off into the evening.

IX. Ad Deum, qui laetificat juventutem meam.

Catherine went inside, directly to the middle room, put her hat and coat away in the closet, and stood for a good while, though she would have been hard put to say afterward how many minutes or what it had been. After, though, she looked down at her hands, still in their beige Lenten gloves, and she stretched all of a sudden, her hands high over her head, her mouth opening up and letting the breath out cavernously, as when she just woke from a long sleep, and then she laughed. She pulled the gloves off and tossed them into the closet on top of her hat, shut the closet door.

She walked through the kitchen and out on to the porch, where she could see from the porch light the top of Petie's head where he sat on the back steps. She opened the porch screen and shut it behind her, went down the steps, and up to the fence.

"Hi," she said.

He looked straight ahead, not at anything, she thought. Those bandages on his head, his left arm covered up to the armpit in a thick white plaster cast, his cut face, none of them hurt her to look at. He was in the same shirt he flung the cats in, and she could smell him where she stood, a warm and sour smell that wasn't bad but not pleasant either, not the smell that to her went with Petie. She waited a few seconds, but he didn't get up and go back in the house.

"Hold up," she said, and she stuck the toe of her foot into one of the squares in the wire fence. She got a hold of the fence post and hoisted herself up, not caring about her dress or if her underpants could be seen by him or anybody else. Her slip got stuck coming down on the other side, but it didn't matter, she pulled at it until it came free.

She sat down next to him on the stairs, he even slid over a little to make room for her. She touched his right hand with her left, and they sat there together, fingers dry, palms moist. They didn't say anything. She couldn't hear him breathe. His hand was light in hers, but not engaged. She was holding on to him.

In the early hours, she had often imagined them in a little cabin in West Virginia, him smiling across the room at her with his bad teeth, the grey lines between the few teeth he had left showing dull but content, and stuffed cats crouched patiently on the wooden mantelpiece. At night they sat in rockers and he told stories to their sons and daughters about the days he used to rule the world from his back yard in the big city. Their round eyes glowed at his voice in the firelight, wild children raised on meat slaughtered on a whirl of air, so pretty.

She thought of this now, but then a siren made Petie's dog howl from inside the house, and his mother called for him to come in to dinner. He pulled his hand away, got up on his own still not making a sound, and went inside without looking at her or saying a thing.

Mr. Emerson came out his back door just then, glass tumbler in hand. He and Catherine looked at each other. She stood but didn't say anything, he spit out of the side of his mouth and sat down. She stayed for another moment or so, still looking at him. She could tell he was pretending she wasn't. She was impressed by the expression of dignity on his face as he ignored her. She heard her mother moving next door, and turned, walked the length of Petie's yard, let herself out of his back gate and into her own, and went in the house.

Acknowledgments

Many thanks to the editors and staff of Apprentice House Press for accepting this work and putting it to print. I am especially grateful to Rachel Kingsley and Alessia Hughes, and thank them for their hard work, professionalism, and many kindnesses.

To my agent, John Sibley Williams, my warmest gratitude for his belief in the book, his unwavering encouragement, and his incredible hard work.

I would like to especially thank Jonis Agee for her patient and always generous support. Thanks to my colleagues at the University of Nebraska-Lincoln, including incomparable readers Christine Harding Thornton and Robert Noel Fuglei. Thanks also to Gayathri Prabhu, Kate Kostelnik, and John Schulze for their encouragement and suggestions.

Many thanks to Mary Helen Stefaniak and Brent Spencer, who commented on sections of the book when it was first finding its way.

Sincere thanks to Ann Pancake and David Huddle for their kindness in reading an early draft of the novel, and for their perceptive comments.

To my sisters, Monica Rose and Cecily Updegraff, my love and thanks. To Jim Madison, a debt of gratitude.

To my husband, Mark Koesters, and our daughter Clare, more love and thanks than I can possibly say. You are the lights I see by.

Finally, this is a work of fiction. As few liberties with history and locale have been taken as possible, but in some instances real places have been substituted with imaginary ones (for example, the synagogue on Lloyd Street is not intended to represent B'nai Israel Synagogue). Other than known historical figures, including Redmund Fitzhugh, the fictional character very loosely based on Clarence "Red" Burman, no representation of persons living or dead should be assumed. The Latin titles to the Palm Sunday sections are taken from the old Roman Catholic liturgy for Palm Sunday. Any errors are unintended and my own.

About the Author

Adrian Gibbons Koesters is a native of Baltimore, where she spent much of her childhood in and around the *Union Square* neighborhood. She has lived for many years in Nebraska, where she is currently the Research Editor for the Vice Chancellor of Research at the University of Nebraska Medical Center in Omaha. Her two volumes of poetry, *Many Parishes* and *Three Days with the Long Moon*, were published by Baltimore's BrickHouse Books, and her short nonfiction work on trauma and prayer, *Healing Mysteries*, was published by Paulist Press. *Union Square* is her first novel.

Apprentice
House Press
Loyola University Maryland

Apprentice House is the country's only campus-based, student-staffed book publishing company. Directed by professors and industry professionals, it is a nonprofit activity of the Communication Department at Loyola University Maryland.

Using state-of-the-art technology and an experiential learning model of education, Apprentice House publishes books in untraditional ways. This dual responsibility as publishers and educators creates an unprecedented collaborative environment among faculty and students, while teaching tomorrow's editors, designers, and marketers.

Outside of class, progress on book projects is carried forth by the AH Book Publishing Club, a co-curricular campus organization supported by Loyola University Maryland's Office of Student Activities.

Eclectic and provocative, Apprentice House titles intend to entertain as well as spark dialogue on a variety of topics. Financial contributions to sustain the press's work are welcomed. Contributions are tax deductible to the fullest extent allowed by the IRS.

To learn more about Apprentice House books or to obtain submission guidelines, please visit www.apprenticehouse.com.

Apprentice House
Communication Department
Loyola University Maryland
4501 N. Charles Street
Baltimore, MD 21210
Ph: 410-617-5265 • Fax: 410-617-2198
info@apprenticehouse.com • www.apprenticehouse.com